The University and its Boundaries

Grounded in key sociological theory on the concepts of boundaries, power and control, this text addresses the question of whether the university is thriving or merely surviving.

Using a sociological lens to consider how institutions must engage in boundary transactions in order to maintain their unique position and identity, this book explores how these transactions also have the potential to undermine academic boundaries. Including a detailed analysis of the activities, organisation and outputs of academic research in the context of science, technology, engineering, mathematics and medicine (STEMM) departments of UK universities, the arguments presented have implications for universities and their stakeholders not only in the United Kingdom, but wherever universities face challenges of purpose and identity, particularly where these are shaped by neoliberal modes of governance and management.

Insights into how universities must balance the ideas of themselves as teaching institutions, research institutions and their broader societal importance and impact make this important reading for higher education scholars and postgraduate students, sociological theorists and all those interested in the future of the university.

Eliel Cohen is a research associate at the Centre for Higher Education Research and Scholarship, Imperial College London, UK.

The University and its Boundaries
Thriving or Surviving in the 21st Century

Eliel Cohen

Routledge
Taylor & Francis Group
LONDON AND NEW YORK

First published 2021
by Routledge
2 Park Square, Milton Park, Abingdon, Oxon OX14 4RN

and by Routledge
52 Vanderbilt Avenue, New York, NY 10017

Routledge is an imprint of the Taylor & Francis Group, an informa business

© 2021 Eliel Cohen

The right of Eliel Cohen to be identified as author of this work has been asserted by him in accordance with sections 77 and 78 of the Copyright, Designs and Patents Act 1988.

All rights reserved. No part of this book may be reprinted or reproduced or utilised in any form or by any electronic, mechanical, or other means, now known or hereafter invented, including photocopying and recording, or in any information storage or retrieval system, without permission in writing from the publishers.

Trademark notice: Product or corporate names may be trademarks or registered trademarks, and are used only for identification and explanation without intent to infringe.

British Library Cataloguing-in-Publication Data
A catalogue record for this book is available from the British Library

Library of Congress Cataloging-in-Publication Data
A catalog record for this book has been requested

ISBN: 978-0-367-56298-4 (hbk)
ISBN: 978-1-003-10295-3 (ebk)

Typeset in Times New Roman
by Apex CoVantage, LLC

Contents

List of figures	vi
List of tables	vii
Acknowledgements	viii
List of abbreviations	ix

1	The university as a bounded institution: thriving or (just) surviving?	1
2	The boundary lens: theorising academic activity	14
3	Zoom in: STEMM research through the boundary lens	42
4	Zoom out: the knowledge society through the boundary lens	63
5	The future of the university and its boundaries	80
	Appendix	98
	Index	102

Figures

3.1	Pie chart showing outreach activities contributing to different missions	52
3.2	Pie chart showing boundary structures contributing to different missions	59
3.3	Pie chart showing boundary-spanning contributing to different missions	61
5.1	Bar chart showing forms of transaction by departmental status	83
5.2	Stacked bar chart showing collaboration with non-doctorate holders by branch of science	87

Tables

2.1 Sampled disciplines and epistemic characteristics   29
3.1 Frequency of cases with collaboration (co-authorship) by 'stage'   54
3.2 Frequency of cases of user-oriented outputs by 'stage'   56

Acknowledgements

I hope all will forgive me for the minimalist approach I have adopted here. From words of encouragement to intensive support; from new opportunities to new ways of thinking; from inherited inquisitiveness to career advice; from duty to friendship; from collegiality to love, I wish to briefly acknowledge the following people, each of whom have contributed in some way to my writing this book (some of whom will likely never read this): Dr Vassiliki Papatsiba; Dr Heather Ellis; Professor James Wilsdon; Professor Geoff Payne; Professor Simon Susen; Dr Sandra Leaton Gray; Dr Fiona Rodger; Dr Clare Brooks; Professor Jackie Leach Scully; Professor Martyn Kingsbury; Professor Richard Watermeyer; Dr Jenn Chubb; Dr Julianne Viola; anonymous reviewers; my generous research participants; Dr Jared Crane; Katie Cohen; Hyeonseon Ro; Audrey Cohen; Stephen Cohen; Isaac Cohen; and Mary Shad.

Abbreviations

CERI	Centre for Educational Research and Innovation
HEFCE	Higher Education Funding Council for England
NERC	Natural Environment Research Council
NHS	National Health Service
OECD	Organisation for Economic Co-operation and Development
REF	Research Excellence Framework
STEMM	Science, Technology, Engineering, Mathematics and Medicine
UoA	Units of Assessment

1 The university as a bounded institution

Thriving or (just) surviving?

Is academia in the twenty-first century thriving? Or is it just, and only just, surviving? On the one hand, academia appears to have thrived in recent years and decades, which have witnessed the proliferation of new specialisms and disciplines and the expansion of universities' scale and scope. A seemingly ever-increasing range and quantity of people and organisations are coming to be associated with the university, whether as students, staff, sponsors, partners or other forms of stakeholders, as governments and societies place great faith in the capacity of academic knowledge to help solve many of its economic, technological, environmental, societal, health and security issues. The notions of academic work and academic identity have themselves expanded to accommodate these developments, with 'entrepreneurial', 'engaged', 'connected' and 'impactful' emerging as new academic modalities.

Yet many believe that academia, far from thriving, is barely surviving. A closer intertwinement with governments and industries is perceived by some not as a display of authentic, autonomous agency, but as symptomatic of a narrow-minded, short-termist and business-like approach to academic work and management which is at odds with traditional academic values. Academic freedom and autonomy, arguably academia's most deeply entrenched values (Russell, 1993), are seen to be challenged on multiple fronts. Support for research increasingly means following the agendas of external actors and interests (particularly those of industry and governments), rather than agendas geared towards scholarship, disciplinarity or theoretical advancement. It also increasingly means accepting judgement according to externally derived criteria, such as 'relevance' and 'impact', which do not necessarily align with other values and criteria, such as creativity, collegiality and rigorous scholarship. And while the *thriving* of universities has led to new, expansive academic identities, the *just surviving* of universities has had an opposite effect. The business-minded and short-term model is perceived to have challenged and undermined traditional values associated with academic identity by leading to an increasing number of academics employed on fixed-term and/or teaching-only contracts, restricting their capacity to exercise autonomy and engage in free and open inquiry and scholarship.

The paradox of the twenty-first-century university, then, is that to thrive it must cross boundaries and be engaged in an increasingly complex, multidimensional and knowledge intensive society (Brennan, Papatsiba, Sousa, & Hoffman, 2016); but that to survive means simultaneously reinforcing the integrity of its own boundaries and 'boundedness' so as not to undermine its distinctive institutional identity and thereby deprive society of its distinctive value and contributions. Amidst these 'competing logics' (Shields & Watermeyer, 2020, p. 13), a key challenge for the university and its stakeholders is to consider what conceptual tools and principles can be used to ensure an appropriate balance between these opposing pressures; in other words, how to secure the university's future as an institution which neither overly strengthens nor overly weakens its boundaries. In this book, I put forward what I call the 'boundary lens' as just such a conceptual tool. I briefly introduce the 'boundary lens' later in this chapter and elaborate on it in Chapter 2. First, I want to add some further context to this 'paradox of the university' with an overview of key developments facing academia in recent decades, including a brief 'policy history' of how these developments have played out in one national context, that of the United Kingdom.

Context: boundary pressures, the 'third mission' and the 'impact agenda'

From at least the early 1980s, academic research and related activities, as well as the governance of academic institutions more generally, have become matters of heightened significance for governments and societies across the globe (Deem, Hillyard, & Reed, 2007; Martin, 2011). This was a time when the importance of academic knowledge for economic competitiveness was starting to become apparent to governments and industries across Europe and America (Centre for Educational Research and Innovation, 1982; Etzkowitz & Leydesdorff, 1995; Martin, 2011; Smith, Ward, & House, 2011), prompting the notion of a 'third mission' for universities (de Jong, Barker, Cox, Sveinsdottir, & Van den Besselaar, 2013; Kitagawa & Lightowler, 2013; Perkmann et al., 2013). In addition to their research and teaching missions, universities were considered to also have a third mission to contribute to the improvement of society more directly through reorientations of their research and teaching and also by using academic knowledge and expertise to engage directly in civil society or the market.

The 1980s also witnessed the emergence of New Public Management that has since characterised institutional governance across many sectors and nations, with a focus on value for money, measured performance and accountability (Clark, 1998, 2004; Deem, 2004; Lambert, 2003; Shattock, 2017; Watermeyer & Olssen, 2016). Under these conditions, academic managers are incentivised and empowered to exert influence on their institutions, whilst autonomy for individual academics 'is . . . secured through compliance with the . . . expectations of their institutions and funders' (Shields & Watermeyer, 2020, p. 12), leading to claims of 'dwindling agency, authority and legitimacy' (Watermeyer, 2019, p. 9). Managerial steering is often geared less towards the creation of conditions for academics to enact traditional values of free and critical inquiry and more towards maximising 'productivity' (Rhoades, 2001, p. 619), narrowly defined in terms of revenue or other indicators measured by national and international assessments and league tables (Deem et al., 2007; Hazelkorn, 2007, 2008; Marginson & van der Wende, 2007).

It is within the international context of the emergence of New Public Management and the notion of a third mission for universities that the UK government introduced a national performance-related research funding system, in which assessments of universities' research 'quality' would significantly determine academic research grant allocations. The first such national assessment was conducted in 1986 and they have since been conducted every three to seven years (with the periods between assessments generally increasing over time). In the 1980s and 1990s, these national assessments of universities' research were focused quite generically on the *quality* rather than the *impact* of research, while scrutiny of the economic impact of research was targeted at research councils rather than universities themselves (Kearnes & Wienroth, 2011; Watermeyer, 2016; see also policy documents, Department for Business Innovation & Skills, 2010; Office of Science and Technology, 1993; Research Councils UK, 2007; Warry, 2006). However, by 2006 the government felt that more direct reforms were needed to reorient academics towards more socially and economically useful research, leading, in 2008, to 'impact' being confirmed as a new element of future research assessments (Department for Education & Skills, 2006; HEFCE, 2009; Smith et al., 2011). The first assessment to include 'impact' was the 2014 run, which had been rebranded as the Research Excellence Framework (REF) and since that time the political emphasis on impact has continued to grow (Wilsdon, 2017), reflected in the decision to increase the weighting of impact from 20% to 25% for the next REF (originally scheduled for 2021 but currently delayed due to the 2019 coronavirus pandemic).

The 'impact agenda' therefore refers to a set of policies and an accompanying discourse which encourage and incentivise academic institutions and researchers to shift focus towards more societally and economically 'relevant' problems (Chubb, Watermeyer, & Wakeling, 2017; Martin, 2011; Smith et al., 2011). The impact agenda is arguably more explicit in the United Kingdom than elsewhere, but similar developments are playing out globally. These conditions operate 'selectively' (Bernstein, 2000, p. 55; Leydesdorff, 2010, p. 370; Robertson, 2010, p. 193) on academic actors, making it possible for academics to achieve distinction (Watermeyer & Chubb, 2019) according to new kinds of criteria and values which derive from or take place amongst 'external publics' (Putnam, 2009, p. 23), thereby challenging academia as a 'bounded' field in which the primary aim of academics is to achieve distinction and prestige amongst themselves (Bourdieu, 1975; Cooper, 2009; Smith et al., 2011; Turnbull & Antalffy, 2009). The result of academics' 'creative engagement with [these] shifting structural conditions' (Cooper, 2009, p. 629) has been that participation in boundary-crossing activities has become not only normalised, but a marker and predictor of academic success (Perkmann et al., 2013; Terama, Smallman, Lock, Johnson, & Austwick, 2016). The systematic study of how academic boundaries are being (re)construed and (re)shaped through interactions across them is therefore significant and timely.

Introducing the 'boundary lens'

Many higher education theorists have adopted the 'boundary' metaphor to make sense of contemporary issues and debates related to the role, organisation, activities and relation of universities. For example, universities' efforts to maintain institutional autonomy and distinctiveness while also attempting to increase their social reach and relevance has been conceptualised in terms of managing and (re)negotiating 'boundaries' (Bacevic, 2019; Hatakenaka, 2004; Henkel, 2007; Kogan, 2005; Nickolai, Hoffman, & Trautner, 2012; Wright, 2016). The metaphor has also been applied to specific developments, for example to the expansion of new kinds of 'boundary-crossing' activities (e.g., outreach and commercialisation), 'boundary structures' (e.g., technology transfer offices and transdisciplinary research centres) and 'boundary-spanning' professional identities (e.g., academic entrepreneurs or 'knowledge brokers') (Cervantes, 2017; Chau, Gilman, & Serbanica, 2017; Koryakina, Sarrico, & Teixeira, 2015; Lam, 2010; Primeri & Reale, 2015).

Theorists have thus been drawn to the boundary metaphor to study both 'process and outcome' (Vakkuri, 2004, p. 17), that is, both *how* academic change takes place and *what* academia is becoming. In this book, I bring these uses of the boundary metaphor into a 'boundary lens', a conceptual tool for analysing these processes and outcomes. To do so, I join other authors (Beck & Young, 2005; Muller & Young, 2019; Nickolai et al., 2012;

Sataøen, 2018) in drawing from the theoretical legacy of Basil Bernstein (2000), who grounds the application of the boundary metaphor within his sociological conceptualisations of 'power' and 'control' over boundary processes and outcomes.

Briefly, following Bernstein (2000), I understand a social boundary as a socially constructed device for regulating a relationship between two or more categories, such as categories of actor or group, or categories of activity or domains of knowledge. For example, the discipline of physics is relatively bounded from that of chemistry or history, and we call those who hold authority over these knowledge domains physicists, chemists and historians. At a higher order, academic knowledge in general is relatively 'bounded' (Bernstein, 2000, p. 99; Henkel, 2004, p. 168; Lam, 2010, p. 333) from non-academic knowledge.

All social boundaries, including academic boundaries, can be understood as a reflection of, and an attempt to preserve, the 'power' held by a given group over some social asset or position, where 'power' is understood as a group's capacity to self-define a domain of authority for itself (Bernstein, 2000) – say authority over knowledge claims related to the physical world or to historical facts and interpretations. They are an 'attempt to regulate those who have access' (Bernstein, 2000, p. 30). In this way, academic boundaries 'are conceptual and normative, as well as organizational. They serve to reinforce identification by highlighting differences from other groups' (Henkel, 2004, p. 168).

Although the power to self-define a domain of authority may, as will be discussed later, sometimes give the appearance of 'insulation' (Bernstein, 2000, p. 6) from the complexities, politics and problems of wider society, in reality this is only a partial insulation. As noted in an insightful OECD Centre for Educational Research and Innovation (CERI, 1982) report, 'even the phenomenon of the "ivory tower" must be understood in terms of interaction, not as a symbol of an illusory independence' (p. 17). This is because no boundary, no matter how powerful and durable, is completely self-sustaining; they always require broader societal legitimacy. Therefore, all bounded groups and categories are under some pressure to show their value to wider society, or at least to some sections of it. Therefore, precisely because academia is interested in maintaining its relatively bounded and powerful position in society, it must actively enter into some form of *relationship* with society, in particular an 'exchange relationship' (Kogan, 2000, p. 215).

In this book, I conceptualise any instance of a group or institution showing its value to wider society as a form of exchange which I call a 'boundary transaction'. They can take many forms. For example, an academic paper or report could constitute a form of boundary transaction if it comes to be taken up in a non-academic context. A graduate who applies their academic skills and training in a non-academic workplace could be another example. Such transactions allow the bounded group (academia) to show its broader social value, thereby contributing to the legitimacy of, and therefore reproduction of, its boundaries. Boundary transactions need not take the form of institutional 'outputs' such as papers and graduates. For example, the appointment of an honorary professor based on their reputation in a non-academic sector fits my definition of a boundary transaction, in the sense that the university bestows symbolic status upon this person, and provides them with the opportunity to shape the educational or research activity of the given university. Organisational structures can also be forms of boundary transaction. For example, the construction of a technology transfer office or new problem-focused research centre may be understood as boundary transactions in and of themselves given that they symbolically signify academia's openness to engage with certain areas of the economy and pressing societal and global problems.

From the perspective of the boundary lens adopted, academia's interest in transactions is the reproduction of its boundaries. By contrast, non-academic actors' interest in transactions is the value and benefit they can receive from the bounded group through these transactions. These different interests do not necessarily stunt or undermine this 'exchange relationship'. Indeed, part of what I am arguing for is the 'acceptance of differentiation and exchange' (Kogan, 2000, p. 207) between academic and non-academic actors. However, these different interests can and sometimes do come into conflict. Boundary transactions *may* serve to reproduce a given bounded category – by virtue of demonstrating the wider societal value that derives from its boundedness – but they may also, over time, act as mechanisms for the 'weakening' (Henkel, 2004, p. 168) of boundaries. If the bounded group becomes overly preoccupied with its external validation and valuation, there is a possibility that its activities, objectives and interests come to be almost identical with those of external actors, thereby losing its distinctive identity and potential value. On the other hand, if a bounded group becomes overly preoccupied with its distinctiveness and freedom from wider societal concerns, it risks becoming irrelevant and, paradoxically, losing its legitimate claims to authority, as other actors and groups will fill the gap left by a distant and disinterested institution. The challenge for universities is therefore not how they can extricate themselves from society, but how to 'ensur[e] that their distinctive missions and competencies are strong so that they can enter into negotiation and partnerships from a position of strength . . . [and] on terms which . . . stand the test of being compatible with . . . academic functions' (Kogan, 2000, pp. 215–216).

The academic enterprise therefore involves a constant interplay of *reinforcing* and *opening up* of academic boundaries. The reinforcement of boundaries is necessary to protect what is distinctive and distinctively valuable about academia, while the opening up or loosening of academic boundaries is necessary to maintain wider societal relevance and legitimacy. This presents an inescapable tension and an ongoing challenge to academic actors, managers and stakeholders, who would seek to preserve or enhance the role and value of academia. Opening up boundaries and increasing boundary-crossing interactions always entails costs and risk, since it has the potential to weaken and undermine the integrity of academic boundaries; and yet it is a risk that cannot be avoided, since crossing boundaries is essential to the fulfilment of academic work and the enactment of academic identity.

Chapter 2 will elaborate on these ideas, particularly the idea that there is a constant interplay of 'power' and 'control' (Bernstein, 2000) between academia and wider society over the 'transactions' across academic boundaries. The boundary lens is a conceptual tool designed to bring into focus the loci of 'control' (Bernstein, 2000) over the terms of exchange (i.e., over boundary transactions) and to enable inferences to be made about the balance of power relations and the state of academic boundaries. In this way, the boundary lens comprises a useful tool and set of concepts for evaluating the state of the university as an institution that is thriving or one that is just surviving.

Aims and overview of the book

My main interest in writing this book is in developing conceptual tools for analysing the role and activities of universities in the twenty-first century, centred around the metaphor of academic 'boundaries', in order to progress the debate about whether the university is an institution that is thriving or one that is just (and only just) surviving. Specifically, I suggest that such research could usefully centre around the investigation of actual instances of boundary-crossing activities and their implications for the reproduction or weakening of academic boundaries. My simplified contention is that where boundary transactions serve as new opportunities for academia's distinctive identity and values to be enacted, then they can be interpreted primarily as forces for reproducing and legitimating academic boundaries. By contrast, where boundary transactions appear to undermine academia's distinctiveness and autonomy, they are contributing to a weakening of academic boundaries.

Chapter 2 (*The Boundary Lens: Theorising Academic Activity*) further develops the key concepts introduced in this chapter, explaining how boundary transactions are key mechanisms in the regulation of universities' role and relations with society, as well as mechanisms for changes to these roles and relations. The final section of Chapter 2 focuses on how the boundary lens could be applied in empirical research, drawing on a study which I conducted, the findings of which inform Chapters 3 and 4.

Chapter 3 (*Zoom In: STEMM Research through the Boundary Lens*) and Chapter 4 (*Zoom Out: The Knowledge Society through the Boundary Lens*) both draw from my empirical research. In order to maximise my understanding of the complex and nuanced functioning and effects of boundary transactions, it was important that I not only analyse boundary transactions themselves, in isolation, but also analyse the complex and multidimensional contexts in which they took place. For example, in order to capture how subtle differences in the epistemic nature of a discipline may influence the functioning and effects of boundary transactions, I only drew on departments from the so-called STEMM disciplines of science, technology, engineering, mathematics and medicine. As others have recognised (Hoffman, 2011; Slaughter & Leslie, 1997; Ylijoki, 2003), limiting the scope of study in this way can make certain kinds of insights more achievable, such as how academic boundaries may be experienced, confronted and crossed differently depending on research 'orientation' (i.e., towards more 'basic' or 'applied' research). I also found that narrowing my research in this way freed me to consider how a range of other factors interrelate at multiple levels to shape the functioning and effects of boundary transactions. As Chapters 3 and 4 will show, these include things like the non-epistemic objectives or motivations for the research (e.g., impact or revenue generation); the wider programmes of research that specific projects and activities contributed to; the sources of demand and funding for the research; the way that the research was organised institutionally; the roles of key researchers; the particular forms that boundary transactions took; and the power/control relations of the academic and non-academic actors between whom the boundary transactions took place.

Lastly, Chapter 5 (*The Future of the University and its Boundaries*) reflects on a tension that is inherent to the academic enterprise. Universities, as relatively distinctive, autonomous and bounded institutions, must engage in boundary transactions in order to maintain their unique position and identity. As shown throughout the book, boundary transactions tend to regulate academic boundaries quite effectively. However, these same transactions also have the potential to undermine academic boundaries. While this tension is not unique to our time, what is perhaps unique is the extent to which universities have become so central to and embedded within a knowledge-intensive society in which academic knowledge has so much to offer to so many competing and sometimes conflicting goals. Although my data generally shows boundary transactions functioning, on balance, to reinforce rather than undermine academic boundaries, I also find evidence that universities' closer integration in markets and in technoscientific systems of power at national and international levels are intensifying the pressures on academic boundaries and may be leading to a shift in control over boundary transactions. I also find evidence of boundaries and boundary transactions being differentially experienced across epistemic and institutional contexts, with these differences not being neutral, but often grounded in differential power and status hierarchies within academia. Chapter 5 concludes by discussing the implications of these insights and findings for policy and action, particularly in relation to the question of how the university's future may be secured as a global institution which neither overly strengthens its boundaries to isolate itself from the world, nor overly weakens its boundaries so as to lose its identity – in other words, of how to attain a sustainable balance of power and control.

References

Bacevic, J. (2019). With or without U? Assemblage theory and (de)territorialising the university. *Globalisation, Societies and Education, 17*(1), 78–91. doi:10.1080/14767724.2018.1498323

Beck, J., & Young, M. (2005). The assault on the professions and the restructuring of academic and professional identities: A Bernsteinian analysis. *British Journal of Sociology of Education, 26*(2), 183–197. doi:10.1080/0142569042000294165

Bernstein, B. (2000). *Pedagogy, symbolic control, and identity: Theory, research, critique* (2nd ed.). Oxford: Rowman & Littlefield.

Bourdieu, P. (1975). The specificity of the scientific field and the social conditions of the progress of reason. *Sociology of Science, 14*, 19–47. doi:10.1177/053901847501400602

Brennan, J., Papatsiba, V., Sousa, S. B., & Hoffman, D. (2016). Diversity of higher education institutions in networked knowledge societies: A comparative examination. In D. M. Hoffman & J. Välimaa (Eds.), *Re-becoming universities?: Higher education institutions in networked knowledge societies*. Dordrecht: Springer.

Centre for Educational Research and Innovation. (1982). *The university and the community: The problems of changing relationships*. Paris: Organisation for Economic Co-operation and Development.

Cervantes, M. (2017). Higher education institutions in the knowledge triangle. *Foresight and STI Governance, 11*(2), 27–42. doi:10.17323/2500-2597.2017.2.27.42

Chau, V. S., Gilman, M., & Serbanica, C. (2017). Aligning university–industry interactions: The role of boundary spanning in intellectual capital transfer. *Technological Forecasting & Social Change, 123*(C), 199–209. doi:10.1016/j.techfore.2016.03.013

Chubb, J., Watermeyer, R., & Wakeling, P. (2017). Fear and loathing in the academy? The role of emotion in response to an impact agenda in the UK and Australia. *Higher Education Research & Development, 36*(3), 555–568. doi:10.1080/07294360.2017.1288709

Clark, B. R. (1998). *Creating entrepreneurial universities: Organizational pathways of transformation.* Oxford: Pergamon Press.

Clark, B. R. (2004). *Sustaining change in universities: Continuities in case studies and concepts.* Maidenhead: Open University Press.

Cooper, M. H. (2009). Commercialization of the university and problem choice by academic biological scientists. *Science, Technology, & Human Values, 34*(5), 629–653. doi:10.1177/0162243908329379

Deem, R. (2004). The knowledge worker, the manager-academic and the contemporary UK university: New and old forms of public management? *Financial Accountability & Management, 20*(2), 107–128. doi:10.1111/j.1468-0408.2004.00189.x

Deem, R., Hillyard, S., & Reed, M. (2007). *Knowledge, higher education, and the new managerialism: The changing management of UK universities.* Oxford: Oxford University Press.

de Jong, S., Barker, K., Cox, D., Sveinsdottir, T., & Van den Besselaar, P. (2013). *Understanding societal impact through studying productive interactions.* Working Paper 1304. Rethenau Institut.

Department for Business Innovation & Skills. (2010). *UK Research Council system: Overview of economic impact.* Retrieved from www.gov.uk/government/publications/uk-research-council-system-overview-of-economic-impact

Department for Education & Skills. (2006). *Reform of higher education research assessment and funding: A consultation.* Retrieved from http://dera.ioe.ac.uk/6140/

Etzkowitz, H., & Leydesdorff, L. (1995). The triple helix – University-industry-government relations: A laboratory for knowledge based economic development. *EASST Review, 14*(1), 14–19. doi:10.1177/0896920510365921

Hatakenaka, S. (2004). *University-industry partnerships in MIT, Cambridge, and Tokyo: Storytelling across boundaries.* New York: Taylor & Francis.

Hazelkorn, E. (2007). The impact of league tables and ranking systems on higher education decision making. *Higher Education Management and Policy, 19*(2), 81–105. doi:10.1787/hemp-v19-art12-en

Hazelkorn, E. (2008). Learning to live with league tables and ranking: The experience of institutional leaders. *Higher Education Policy, 21*(2), 193–215. doi:10.1057/hep.2008.1

Henkel, M. (2004). Current science policies and their implications for the formation and maintenance of academic identity. *Higher Education Policy, 17*(2), 167. doi:10.1057/palgrave.hep.8300049

Henkel, M. (2007). Can academic autonomy survive in the knowledge society? A perspective from Britain. *Higher Education Research & Development*, 87–99. doi:10.1080/07294360601166836

Higher Education Funding Council for England. (2009). *Research Excellence Framework: Second consultation on the assessment and funding of research.* Retrieved from http://dera.ioe.ac.uk/9288/

Hoffman, S. G. (2011). The new tools of the science trade: Contested knowledge production and the conceptual vocabularies of academic capitalism. *Social Anthropology, 19*(4), 439–462. doi:10.1111/j.1469-8676.2011.00180.x

Kearnes, M., & Wienroth, M. (2011). Tools of the trade: UK research intermediaries and the politics of impacts. *Minerva, 49*(2), 153–174. doi:10.1007/s11024-011-9172-4

Kitagawa, F., & Lightowler, C. (2013). Knowledge exchange: A comparison of policies, strategies, and funding incentives in English and Scottish higher education. *Research Evaluation, 22*(1), 1–14. doi:10.1093/reseval/rvs035

Kogan, M. (2000). Higher education communities and academic identity. *Higher Education Quarterly, 54*(3), 207–216. doi:10.1111/1468-2273.00156

Kogan, M. (2005). Modes of knowledge and patterns of power. *The International Journal of Higher Education and Educational Planning, 49*(1–2), 9–30. doi:10.1007/s10734-004-2911-9

Koryakina, T., Sarrico, C., & Teixeira, P. (2015). Universities' third mission activities: Challenges to extending boundaries. In E. Primeri & E. Reale (Eds.), *The transformation of university institutional and organizational boundaries: Organizational boundaries*. Rotterdam: Sense.

Lam, A. (2010). From 'ivory tower traditionalists' to 'entrepreneurial scientists'?: Academic scientists in fuzzy university–industry boundaries. *Social Studies of Science, 40*(2), 307–340. doi:10.1177/0306312709349963

Lambert, R. (2003). *Lambert review of business-university collaboration: Final report*. University of Illinois at Urbana-Champaign's Academy for Entrepreneurial Leadership Historical Research Reference in Entrepreneurship.

Leydesdorff, L. (2010). The knowledge-based economy and the triple helix model. *Annual Review of Information Science and Technology, 44*(1), 365–417. doi:10.1002/aris.2010.1440440116

Marginson, S., & van der Wende, M. (2007). To rank or to be ranked: The impact of global rankings in higher education. *Journal of Studies in International Education, 11*, 306–304), 306–329. doi:10.1177/1028315307303544

Martin, B. R. (2011). The Research Excellence Framework and the 'impact agenda': Are we creating a Frankenstein monster? *Research Evaluation, 20*(3), 247–254. doi:10.3152/095820211x13118583635693

Muller, J., & Young, M. (2019). Knowledge, power and powerful knowledge revisited. *The Curriculum Journal, 30*(2), 196–214. doi:10.1080/09585176.2019.157029

Nickolai, D. H., Hoffman, S. G., & Trautner, M. N. (2012). Can a knowledge sanctuary also be an economic engine? The marketization of higher education as institutional boundary work. *Sociology Compass, 6*(3), 205–218. doi:10.1111/j.1751-9020.2011.00449.x

Office of Science and Technology. (1993). *Realising our potential: A strategy for science, engineering and technology*. Retrieved from www.gov.uk/government/publications/realising-our-potential-a-strategy-for-science-engineering-and-technology

Perkmann, M., Tartari, V., McKelvey, M., Autio, E., Brostrom, A., D'Este, P., . . . Sobrero, M. (2013). Academic engagement and commercialisation: A review of the literature on university-industry relations. *Research Policy, 42*(2), 423–442. doi:10.1016/j.respol.2012.09.007

Primeri, E., & Reale, E. (Eds.). (2015). *The transformation of university institutional and organizational boundaries: Organizational boundaries*. Rotterdam: Sense Publishers.

Putnam, L. L. (2009). Symbolic capital and academic fields. *Management Communication Quarterly, 23*(1), 127–134. doi:10.1177/0893318909335420

Research Councils UK. (2007). *Increasing the economic impact of the research councils*. Retrieved from www.rcuk.ac.uk/Publications/archive/Increasingei/
Rhoades, G. (2001). Managing productivity in an academic institution: Rethinking the whom, which, what, and whose of productivity. *Research in Higher Education, 42*(5), 619–632. doi:10.1023/A:1011006511651
Robertson, S. L. (2010). Corporatisation, competitiveness, commercialisation: New logics in the globalising of UK higher education. *Globalisation, Societies and Education, 8*(2), 191–203. doi:10.1080/14767721003776320
Russell, C. (1993). *Academic freedom*. London: Routledge.
Sataøen, H. L. (2018). Transforming the "third mission" in Norwegian higher education institutions: A boundary object theory approach. *Scandinavian Journal of Educational Research, 62*(1), 52–67. doi:10.1080/00313831.2016.1212253
Shattock, M. (2017). *University governance in flux. The impact of external and internal pressures on the distribution of authority within British universities: A synoptic view*. Working Paper 13. Retrieved from www.researchcghe.org/publications/university-governance-in-flux-the-impact-of-external-and-internal-pressures-on-the-distribution-of-authority-within-british-universities-a-synoptic-view/
Shields, R., & Watermeyer, R. (2020). Competing institutional logics in universities in the United Kingdom: Schism in the church of reason. *Studies in Higher Education, 45*(1), 3–17. doi:10.1080/03075079.2018.1504910
Slaughter, S., & Leslie, L. L. (1997). *Academic capitalism: Politics, policies, and the entrepreneurial university*. London: Johns Hopkins University Press.
Smith, S., Ward, V., & House, A. (2011). 'Impact' in the proposals for the UK's Research Excellence Framework: Shifting the boundaries of academic autonomy. *Research Policy, 40*(10), 1369–1379. doi:10.1016/j.respol.2011.05.026
Terama, E., Smallman, M., Lock, S., Johnson, C., & Austwick, M. (2016). Beyond academia – Interrogating research impact in the Research Excellence Framework. *PLOS One*. doi:10.1371/journal.pone.0168533
Turnbull, N., & Antalffy, N. (2009). Bourdieu's distinction between philosophical and sociological approaches to Science Studies*. *Sociological Review, 57*(4), 547–566. doi:10.1111/j.1467-954X.2009.01861.x
Vakkuri, J. (2004). Institutional change of universities as a problem of evolving boundaries. *Higher Education Policy, 17*(3), 287–309. doi:10.1057/palgrave.hep.8300056
Warry, P. (2006). Increasing the economic impact of research councils: Advice to the Director General of Science and Innovation, *DTI from the Research Council Economic Impact Group*. Retrieved from https://webarchive.nationalarchives.gov.uk/20070628230000/http://www.dti.gov.uk/files/file32802.pdf
Watermeyer, R. (2016). Impact in the REF: Issues and obstacles. *Studies in Higher Education, 41*(2), 199–214. doi:10.1080/03075079.2014.915303
Watermeyer, R. (2019). *Competitive accountability in academic life: The struggle for social impact and public legitimacy*. Cheltenham: Edward Elgar Publishing.
Watermeyer, R., & Chubb, J. (2019). Evaluating 'impact' in the UK's Research Excellence Framework (REF): Liminality, looseness and new modalities of scholarly distinction. *Studies in Higher Education, 44*(9), 1554–1556. doi:10.1080/03075079.2018.1455082

Watermeyer, R., & Olssen, M. (2016). 'Excellence' and exclusion: The individual costs of institutional competitiveness. *A Review of Science, Learning and Policy, 54*(2), 201–218. doi:10.1007/s11024-016-9298-5

Wilsdon, J. (2017). *REF just got real: Mist now clearing on the road to 2021*. Retrieved from https://wonkhe.com/blogs/ref-just-got-real-ref2021/

Wright, S. (2016). Universities in a knowledge economy or ecology? Policy, contestation and abjection. *Critical Policy Studies, 10*(1), 59–78. doi:10.1080/1946 0171.2016.1142457

Ylijoki, O.-H. (2003). Entangled in academic capitalism? A case-study on changing ideals and practices of university research. *Higher Education, 45*(3), 307–335. doi:10.1023/A:1022667923715

2 The boundary lens
Theorising academic activity

Boundaries in sociological perspective: Bernstein's notion of power

Social boundaries are socially constructed devices for regulating a relationship between two (or potentially more) categories, such as two categories of actor or group, or categories of activity or domains of knowledge. Boundaries reflect and aim to preserve the 'power' (Bernstein, 2000) held by a given group over some privileged social asset or position. Such power, and the ability to reap advantages from it, such as advantages in the form of symbolic and social capital, are scarce. As with anything which is relatively scarce and valuable, its distribution is a social problem, that is, it is an issue which is to be decided through social processes, social mechanisms and the construction of social institutions and norms. The social structures, groupings and norms which arise as a result of struggles to solidify the access to such scarce resources can therefore be thought of as social solutions to socially faced problems (Tilly, 1998).

Boundaries can exist wherever sufficiently powerful actors or groups have a stake in their production and maintenance, that is, whenever sufficiently powerful groups are sufficiently motivated to 'regulate' (Bernstein, 2003/1990, p. 95) the relation between two or more categories. A boundary implies that there is something worth regulating and, therefore, potentially worth struggling over: the definition and demarcation of a 'boundary'; what counts as 'inside' or 'outside'; characteristics such as the 'strength', 'porosity' and 'flexibility' of a boundary – all these are potential sites and sources of struggle, because something about that boundary has value to one or more groups.

Social boundaries do not have to refer to boundaries between groups but can refer to boundaries and divisions between any meaningful 'categories' (Bernstein, 2000, p. 6). However, where the boundary is not between two (or more) well-defined 'groups', it is still likely to be the case that some group has a particular stake in the maintenance of that category. For example, the discipline of physics is a category related to knowledge about certain natural phenomena, but there is also a group, referred to as physicists, who are defined by their authority over that domain of knowledge, and therefore with the greatest interests in the maintenance of the boundaries associated with their discipline.

Boundaries may or may not be formal or legal boundaries. They may rather be based more on norms, expectations and patterns of activity. There may also be a blend of formal and informal regulations. For example, while there may be no formal rules preventing the historian from making claims to knowledge of physics, there are formal bureaucratic realities which classify academic expertise, for example, job titles.

In general, the existence of boundaries and the 'power' which boundaries reflect are not inherently negative or positive. However, they are always *productive*, in the earlier sense that they 'solve' (albeit not necessarily indefinitely) socially faced problems. This 'productive' element even goes for instances in which boundaries have horrific consequences for humanity. For example, in his study of the history of racial segregation in South Africa and the United States, John W. Cell (1982) explains that the concept of segregation emerged not at a time when there was a genuine segregation, that is, a genuine separation between the two 'races'; rather, segregation as a policy, and even usage of the term itself, only emerged when the level of interaction between the two 'races' made acute the problem of regulating their interrelationship. Cell's (1982) perspective therefore sees *segregation* as a special form of *integration*, one that is based on heavily regulated boundaries (regulated by both law and racist ideology).

Coming back to the example of the discipline of physics, boundaries can also be productive in that there can be benefits from allowing distinct and bounded categories 'a space in which to develop their unique[ness]' (Bernstein, 2000, p. 6). The construction and maintenance of boundaries around this domain of knowledge allows a space for dedicated specialisms to develop in which knowledge of the physical world can advance, and new physicists can be trained. Even in such benign and positive cases though, boundaries may still be conceived as having constraining effects, for example where academic disciplines are construed as obsolete structures serving powered academic interests and as preventing, say, physicists, from engaging in the kinds of learning and collaboration that allows them to put their knowledge to use in applied contexts (Krishnan, 2009; McNie, Parris, & Sarewitz, 2016).

For Bernstein, it is ultimately 'power' that determines the strength of a boundary: '*the distribution of power maintains itself essentially through the maintenance of the appropriate degree of insulation between the categories . . . it legitimizes*' (Bernstein, 2003/1990, p. 95, original emphasis). In short, the reproduction or increase in the insulation and strength of academic boundaries reflects the internal power of the bounded group, or the group which has authority over the bounded category (i.e., domain of knowledge or activity). By contrast, a weakening of boundaries reflects that the power of this group has waned relative to outside actors, who either aim to hold authority over that category themselves, or else wish to exert influence over the group that holds authority.

Just as there is no such thing as incontrovertible, unchallengeable power, there is no such thing as a perfectly bounded category. There must always be some form of relation, something that the continued existence and legitimacy of a boundary *gives* to wider society. I have called this a 'transaction' and will take this concept up further next.

Boundary transactions: Bernstein's notion of control

Boundary transactions are interactions between a bounded group (or a group which identifies with some bounded category, in the way that physicists are identified with the bounded discipline of physics) and some other group beyond that boundary which may have an impact on that boundary. As discussed earlier, boundary transactions are unavoidable for the reproduction of boundaries. Another useful concept is that of 'transaction costs', referring to the effort or 'energy expended' in any 'interchange' between actors (Tilly, 1998, p. 53). In general, individuals, organisations and institutions prefer to minimise their transaction costs, which they do in two main ways (Muellerleile & Lewis, 2019; North, 1990). One is to reduce the frequency of interactions, particularly interactions where transacting is relatively costly. An extreme version of this is the 'ivory tower' approach. Crucial to understanding the boundary lens presented in this book is understanding that an 'ivory tower' model for the university, in which the university attempts to strengthen its boundedness from wider society, should not be considered an attempt at *genuine* isolation or full boundedness, free from the need to transact. Rather, it is an attempt at imposing a particular, highly uneven relationship, where all the power lies with the university, the reproduction of which would lie less in transacting actual benefits to external actors, and more in the purely symbolic transaction associated with the university's status as society's prime knowledge institution (Bernstein, 2000; CERI, 1982; Nickolai, Hoffman, & Trautner, 2012). Such a model is risky for the university in the long term, since it leaves open the possibility that other knowledge-based institutions may gain in ascendency by 'transacting' knowledge and knowledge-based outputs in more innovative and interventionist ways which society sees as more valuable than that transacted by an 'ivory tower' institution.

The alternative approach is to open up and to develop close relationships so that communications and 'transactions' between certain actors become normalised, simplified and relatively uncostly. Generally, the greater the demand and reward for certain transactions, the greater the incentive for universities to seek new ways to simplify and improve communications with, align values with and formalise relationships with key transaction partners (North, 1990; Tilly, 1998). Under low(er)-cost transaction conditions, significant communicative efficiencies co-develop with a shared culture and identity through what Bernstein (2000, p. 183) terms 'restricted' code, that is, the shortened forms of communication exhibited within a group of people who can take for granted a significant amount of shared prior knowledge and understanding. By contrast, boundary-crossing often requires the use of 'elaborating' code (Bernstein, 2000, p. 183) – the extended and/or simplified terminology which characterises 'the process of making the meaning available to others not currently "in the know"' (Moore, 2013, pp. 67–68). This would also include cases where shared meaning must be established for collaborative purposes, for example, an interdisciplinary or academic-industry research collaboration, where either one or both parties may need to *elaborate* meaning to the other. Yet this approach can be a risk to the university's distinctive identity and value. The implication is, therefore, that there is a balance to be struck between being sufficiently bounded so as to retain what is distinctive, and distinctively valuable, about the university, whilst being sufficiently open so as to ensure potential real-world benefits are realised and the university's role and value is widely perceived.

Thus, surviving, let alone thriving, depends on at least some form of boundary transactions taking place, and requires that some transaction costs be incurred. Any costs and 'boundary maintenance issues' (Kantasalmi & Tuunainen, 2018, p. 354) must be addressed head-on. It is likely that such issues can often be managed, since bounded groups/categories are normally able to exert a certain amount of 'control' (Bernstein, 2000) over their boundary transactions and 'transaction costs' and thereby regulate their relations to wider society. However, it is important to be aware of how 'control' over boundary transactions can vary, even when the 'forms' (Bernstein, 2000, p. 5) that transactions take appear to be similar.

For example, as mentioned in Chapter 1, any academic output, such as a research publication or a graduate, can be conceptualised as a transaction, since they bring something from within the academic boundary to a context beyond that boundary. There are a broad range of forms that outputs can take and, in any given case, the particular form is influenced by the levels of control exerted by different actors/groups. Research outputs published in academic journals and written in a highly technical form targeted at an audience with significant prior knowledge indicates that 'control' over that output lay *within* the boundaries of academia. By contrast, a research output which took the form of, say, a workshop aimed at non-specialist practitioners or policymakers for whom certain aspects of the research may be useful (McNie et al., 2016) would indicate that greater control lay beyond academic boundaries, say, with the users of the research. To continue the other example of an output, that of a university graduate, where a student's higher education consisted of strongly academic, discipline-specific training, this could be conceptualised as a transaction over which academia held significant control. By contrast, where curricula were designed to promote more 'generic' skills (Bernstein, 2000, p. 53; see also Beck & Young, 2005, p. 189) such as employability, or where curricula were designed with input from relevant industry representatives and potential employers of graduates, this could be conceptualised as a transaction over which there was relative external control.

To summarise, control is closely related to power: 'Control carries the boundary relations of power' (Bernstein, 2000, p. 5). The reproduction of boundaries, that is, the reproduction of the power of bounded categories, therefore depends in significant part on control over boundary transactions. The maintenance of the bounded category depends on the effectiveness of the regulation and control of these transactions such that they reinforce the bounded category's distinctive identity and value to wider society. As such, boundary transactions *may* serve to reproduce a given boundary, but they may also, over time, act as mechanisms for the 'weakening' (Henkel, 2004, p. 168) of boundaries: 'control is double faced for it carries both the power of reproduction and the potential for its change' (Bernstein, 2000, p. 5).

A literature review of academic boundary transactions: forms and effects

In Chapter 1 I discussed the contemporary policy context and was able to frame this partly in terms of boundary pressures. Having discussed the boundary lens in more substantial detail, I now provide a more systematic discussion of the recent trajectory of academic boundaries. I structure the discussion around five main forms of boundary transactions that emerge from the literature: *outreach, collaborative research, user-oriented outputs, boundary structures* and *boundary-spanners*. As well as providing insight into the contemporary state of academic boundaries, I also provide some detail into how each form of boundary transaction functions, including how tensions inhere within each of them, since all forms of transaction may, in theory, contribute towards the strengthening or the weakening of academic boundaries. More in-depth accounts of how each form of boundary transaction operates are provided in Chapter 3 with reference to my own empirical study. I stress that, in reality, the different forms of boundary transaction often overlap and there are many interrelations between the activities, their drivers and their effects, so my classification into five forms of transaction is partly heuristic.

1. 'Outreach' and the origin of the third mission

Outreach refers to participation in and generation of networks with potential users, beneficiaries and stakeholders. In the early 1980s, 'outreach' came to the fore as the core element of the imperative towards a 'third mission' for universities (Benneworth & Charles, 2013; Jongbloed, Enders, & Salerno, 2008; Vakkuri, 2004; Zomer & Benneworth, 2011). Outreach would allow universities to tap into the needs and demands of potential users, and to generate the networks and relationships necessary for enabling effective dissemination and application of academic research and for instigating further and potentially more varied and intensive boundary transactions in the future.

However, as Vakkuri (2004) notes, this 'outreach' imperative was not simply 'imposed on universities' from beyond, but was what he calls a proactive 'boundary enactment transaction', that is, a deliberate attempt by some universities to favourably mould their environments and their role within them (p. 294). Indeed, the early calls for universities to increase their outreach (e.g., CERI, 1982) were themselves influenced by the outreach activities that a few European universities were already experimenting with in the hope of generating local economic benefits and attracting financial support from new potential sponsors. Academics have been 'active agents seeking to shape the boundary between science and business [etc.]' (Lam, 2015, p. 2), and seeing outreach and the third mission as an opportunity to 'mobilize . . . interest in their research' (Benneworth, De Boer, & Jongbloed, 2015, p. 288). They engage in 'transepistemic relations' beyond the 'boundaries of a scientific community' (Knorr-Cetina, 1983, pp. 132–133) in attempts to influence and to account for the interests of potential grant agencies, industry representatives and other stakeholders. Outreach is therefore not only about transmitting knowledge to potential users, but about bringing academics into a boundary-crossing 'dialogical space' where they 'negotiate the social demand for particular types of scientific knowledge, [and] contest political and economic constraints on their research agenda' (Smith, Ward, & House, 2011, p. 1377).

While the outreach imperative may occasionally feel like an unwelcome encroachment or demand to cross academic boundaries on terms not of academics' choosing, it is also an important part of how academia's distinctive identity and boundedness is legitimised and sustained.

2. 'Collaborative research' and the interdependencies and blurring of knowledge sectors

Collaborative knowledge production activities between academic and other non-academic, knowledge-intensive sectors and organisations are increasingly common. It is helpful to locate this form of boundary transaction within the context of increasing interdependencies between different knowledge sectors (Leydesdorff & Etzkowitz, 2001; Petersen, Rotolo, & Leydesdorff, 2016). Academic and non-academic knowledge-intensive sectors are increasingly seen 'as overlapping and interacting systems, with the former augmenting the capacity of the latter to solve an increasing range of complex problems' (Pavitt, 1998, p. 796). The same demands of a third mission for and impact from academic research that underpinned outreach (discussed earlier) have also led to new kinds of expectations about the objectives, modes and even epistemologies of academic research, in that they are to become more like industrial, market-focused research. For example, research has shown (i) that academics experience significant pressure 'to demonstrate excellence in two research ventures, fundamental *and* commercial' (Slaughter & Leslie, 1997, p. 20, original emphasis); (ii) that these pressures can 'persuade some faculty members to change the focus of their laboratories' (Cantwell, 2015, p. 495) towards projects aimed at maximising revenue-generation rather than fundamental learning; and (iii) that the strategies and practices established under these conditions involve a 'micro-level' (Cantwell, 2015, p. 488) complex of inputs and outputs which integrate knowledge, people and technologies in new ways which reshape the system from the bottom up in the likeness of a commercial setting.

Other research has been able to go into even greater depth in analysing how interdependencies with non-academic knowledge-intensive sectors are causing academics to rethink how they construe the epistemic content of their research. One example is Hoffman's (2011) ethnographic study of a computer science department. He found that some academic scientists' consideration of users did not merely mean shifting the topics of study or soliciting the needs of users to ensure outputs were relevant and usable, but became intertwined with epistemology. These academics 'believed that knowing a lot about users was *the* central pillar of scientific discovery' (Hoffman, 2011, p. 453, original emphasis). In another example, identified by W. C. Clark et al. (2016), scientists were forced to rethink and adjust their epistemology when co-producing knowledge with agriculture practitioners. One of the main points of incompatibility causing this re-think was the different conceptions, perceptions and implications of 'uncertainty' estimates (Clark et al., 2016, p. 4621) held by scientists and practitioners: what counts as a reasonable amount of uncertainty, how different levels of uncertainty affect the knowledge claims that can be made, and how to proceed having ascertained the level of uncertainty, all can be understood differently by scientists and practitioners (McNie et al., 2016). Even where research is not oriented towards industry or commerce, it is often no longer sufficient for academic epistemologies to be scientifically rigorous – 'knowledge also needs to be "socially robust", because its validity is no longer determined solely, or predominantly, by narrowly circumscribed scientific communities, but by much wider communities of engagement comprising knowledge producers, disseminators, traders, and users' (Nowotny, Scott, & Gibbons, 2003, pp. 191–192).

The extent of this transformation has persuaded some that we have now entered an 'academic capitalist' system (Slaughter & Leslie, 1997; Slaughter & Rhoades, 2010) and prompted concerns about an age of 'postacademic science' (Ziman, 1996) where there is no discernible distinction between the epistemologies and objectives of academic research and those of industry. Such a view, while extreme, is partly borne out in some of the studies described earlier.

However, it is also important to note that this 'blurring' of boundaries has not been all one way; there is evidence of non-academic sectors taking on some of the roles and interests traditionally associated with academia, such as an interest in conceptualising, sponsoring and even conducting basic research, and it is not always clear whether one is witnessing academic boundaries being encroached on from outside, or whether academia is extending its boundaries and its values on other sectors (Callon, 1994; Etzkowitz, 2008; Etzkowitz & Leydesdorff, 1995; Gibbons et al., 1994).

Either way, the literature highlights that boundary transactions which take the form of inter-sector collaborative activities can be intensive and potentially costly and risky vis-à-vis academic boundaries, as they contribute to growing interdependencies and increased blurring between sectors. But while some academics may wish that academic and non-academic science could stay on separate trajectories, many, including some interviewed for my study, find that collaborating with non-academic actors is both liberating and productive, as they get access to new and pressing problems to solve, as well as resources with which to solve them (Hoffman, 2011; Hughes et al., 2016; Morgan Jones, Manville, & Chataway, 2017).

3. 'User-oriented outputs' as potential 'boundary objects'

As well as outreach and collaboration, the outputs of academic research themselves can be conceptualised as boundary transactions. Examples include 'reports, models . . . [and] standards' (Clark et al., 2016, p. 4615) as well as technological outputs such as instrumentation or software (Nowotny, 2005). While these outputs tend to involve transactions between academia and professional users such as practitioners or policy actors, some outputs bring academia more directly into new spaces, for example, when academics patent research for the market.

A key issue from the perspective of academic boundaries is whether such outputs are simply for the benefit of the recipient, or whether such outputs can be conceptualised as 'boundary objects' (Sataøen, 2018; Star & Griesemer, 1989), in the sense that they provide value and meaning to actors or groups on *both* sides of the boundary, whilst being 'robust enough to maintain identity across them' (Star & Griesemer, 1989, p. 387) – that is, distinct and bounded groups jointly find meaning in the objects in a way that enables each to advance their own objectives and interests. For instance, a scientific paper adopting 'restricted code' (Bernstein, 2000), full of specialist, esoteric language and symbols and targeted at similarly trained experts, would be unlikely to be regarded as a boundary object. By contrast, a paper published in a user-focused form and adopting 'elaborated' or 'elaborating code' (Bernstein, 2000), with all key technical terms and concepts sufficiently explained so that their relevance for user groups and other non-scientific stakeholders is made clear, is more likely to act as a boundary object. So too could specifications of guidelines which, although based on rigorous underpinning scientific research and theory, are presented according to technical standards of relevant professional practitioners rather than only academic scientists. Technologies may also be boundary objects, as when the same technologies sold to industries can also be used to advance basic research. Again, instances of all these examples were found in my study.

Whether or not outputs act as a boundary object, offering meaning and value to parties on either side of the boundary, depends also on social contexts and social relations, as the research of Slaughter, Archerd and Campbell (2004) has shown. They analysed academia-industry collaborations, focusing on issues of 'boundary maintenance' and the 'disputes' that arise as academics 'negotiate these new boundaries' (Slaughter et al., 2004, p. 132). The authors found that, depending on social contexts and relations and individuals' perspectives, the same outputs could become either boundary objects or sources of dispute. For example, research publications could be a source of dispute when perceived by industry collaborators to have no relevance to their goals; while patents could be a source of dispute when seen by academics purely as a means to own and commodify knowledge. However, where industry came to see publications as part of the essential process of advancing knowledge, publications could come to operate as boundary objects. Similarly, where academics came to see patents as part of a process whereby a business model based on intellectual property could yield benefits to the academic's own 'core' missions, that is, their own research agenda, students and institutions, as well as yielding benefits to wider society in the long term, patents too could operate as boundary objects.

Thus, while outputs always have the potential to contribute to the legitimacy of academic boundaries by highlighting some distinctive value of academic research, it may also be possible for outputs to be generated under conditions which undermine academic values and boundaries.

4. *'Boundary structures' and the challenge to disciplinarity*

A range of 'boundary structures' (Chau, Gilman, & Serbanica, 2017, p. 200) or 'boundary organization[s]' (Guston, 1999, p. 88) have been identified which serve to link universities to collaborators, users, beneficiaries and markets. Boundary structures have long been recognised as important for universities' third mission. CERI (1982) favourably highlighted examples of what they refer to as 'horizontal or transversal structures' (p. 43), arguably the first form of which were 'the so-called science shops in The Netherlands in the 1970s . . . [which] linked university researchers to civil society organisations in a broader attempt to democratize both science and society' (Taheri & van Geenhuizen, 2016, p. 32). Regional 'university centers' (Vakkuri, 2004, p. 301; see also Lähteenmäki-Smith, 2014; Variainen & Viiri, 2005), such as found in Finland, continue this explicit third mission goal, partnering with other organisations to bring certain academic activities and offerings to regions without a university. Other sociological studies of universities have revealed the 'outward-facing centres' (Clark, 1998, p. 6) driving the 'entrepreneurial university', and the 'interstitial' or 'intermediate' organisations (Slaughter & Rhoades, 2010, p. 1) which are 'key elements . . . of academic capitalism . . . blur[ring] the boundaries between markets, state, and universities' (Kaidesoja & Kauppinen, 2014, p. 178).

Boundary structures linking universities to markets, such as technology or knowledge transfer offices, science parks and incubators to support academic spin-out companies, have attracted most attention in the literature (Chau et al., 2017). They support the kinds of 'collaboration' and 'outputs' already discussed. Less frequently discussed, but with potentially greater consequences for academic research activity, given the way that they compete with traditional departments as a 'major way to group academic work' (Clark, 1998, p. 6; see also Ponomariov & Boardman, 2010), are problem-centred research centres.

Academics have traditionally been coordinated through academic disciplines. By contrast, problem-oriented research centres operate as interdisciplinary or transdisciplinary units, linking academia to society in the sense that they coordinate academic researchers according to their potential relevance to solving external, non-academic problems, such as the development of 'greener' industrial processes, reducing the human impact on natural life and environments, and using technology to maximise the clinical use of inpatient data (to take a few examples from my own research).

In recent decades, disciplinarity as a mode of integrating academic researchers and advancing knowledge has come under scrutiny with the rise of the third mission, the impact agenda and neoliberal forms of academic management and policy (Gibbons et al., 1994; Krishnan, 2009; Olssen, 2011; Watermeyer & Olssen, 2016). Nearly four decades ago, CERI (1982) described disciplines as not only 'scientific realities but also social institutions which define a sharing of knowledge or of power' (p. 137). For B. R. Clark (2008):

> Disciplines have conscious goals. In fact it is their intentions and strivings and not those stated as the broad aims of higher education which determine the real goals of the many departments, schools, and subcolleges that make up the operating levels of universities.
>
> (p. 285)

To counter this, inter- or transdisciplinarity is seen by some as a solution to problems of the relations not only between bodies of knowledge, but between science and society more generally (Barry & Born, 2013). New research units grounded on 'ideas of interdisciplinarity and transdisciplinarity' aim to promote 'boundary transgressions, in which the disciplinary and disciplining rules, trainings and subjectivities given by existing knowledge corpuses are put aside or superseded' (Barry, Born, & Weszkalnys, 2008, p. 21). Transdisciplinarity implies a 'transcendence of disciplinary norms . . . in the pursuit of . . . real-world problem-solving, or . . . overcoming the distance between specialized and lay knowledges' (Barry et al., 2008, p. 27). As such, it 'does not respect institutional boundaries' (Nowotny, 2006, p. 2). It is practical problems generated beyond academic boundaries, rather than disciplinary ones generated within academic boundaries, that are the main driver and basis for coordination of academic effort and expertise (Nowotny et al., 2003). In this context, new forms of academic organisational structure are 'created on the basis of demands from society more than internal institutionalized norms such as professional or disciplinary' (Nyhagen & Baschung, 2013, pp. 410–411).

These developments arguably reflect a 'weakening' of boundaries and 'greater external dependency' (Bernstein, 2000, p. 52). However, boundary structures, in facilitating boundary transactions, may also have a role in reinforcing and reproducing certain aspects of academic boundaries. For example, transdisciplinarity, rather than implying or leading to '*postdisciplinarity*'

(Bhaskar, 2010, p. 5, original emphasis), often assumes and requires *disciplinary* expertise and knowledge from which to draw. And to that extent, it arguably provides support for a continuation of at least some aspects of academia's traditional shape, for example, an education based on boundaries between disciplines and between disciplinary and non-disciplinary concerns. Moreover, from the perspective of what Durkheim (2013) referred to as the university's 'ideal' to comprise 'a totality or even the totality of the branches of human learning' (p. 93), any novel insights attained by transdisciplinary structures may be interpreted as in keeping with, rather than necessarily challenging, traditional academic objectives. Furthermore, boundary structures have historically often played important roles in raising the profile and prestige of academia because they provide powerful synergies between several of its inward-facing and outward-facing missions (Ben-David, 1971, 1977; Clark, 1989, 1995; Perkin, 1984): they can advance new areas of research and therefore also the interests and careers of academics; they can address the needs of non-academic stakeholders and users; their orientation towards real-world problems provides new learning opportunities for students, thereby advancing universities' other 'core' mission of enhancing the education and employability of its students. My own study finds and discusses examples of just such synergies.

5. *'Boundary-spanners' and tacit knowledge*

I have already discussed how boundary transactions may be enacted through the (co-)production of 'boundary objects', primarily in the form of written or technological outputs and outcomes of research. One of the restrictive features of boundary objects is that they are relatively fixed. Although they can be open to different interpretations, and this is an essential feature of their effectiveness, the shared knowledge and meaning codified within an object is, by its nature, relatively inflexible. But, as shown by chemist and philosopher Michael Polanyi (1962), much knowledge is 'tacit' and not easily transferred through codified objects. As such, any attempt to 'modify' knowledge or 'meaning', say in the process of translating or applying academic knowledge to contexts of application, is, at root, 'a tacit . . . heuristic feat', and therefore also distinctly 'personal' (Polanyi, 1998, p. 111). Indeed, research in the innovation and economic literature suggests that 'the main practical benefits of academic research' are not the research outputs but rather the 'tacit (i.e., non-codifiable) knowledge through personal mobility and face-to-face interaction' (Pavitt, 1998, p. 797; see also Lam, 2007). Moreover, the more tacit the knowledge, the greater the need for strong social ties and 'frequent contacts' (Sousa-Ginel, Franco-Leal, & Camelo-Ordaz, 2017, p. 1138).

All this puts a premium on so-called boundary-spanning individuals (Taheri & van Geenhuizen, 2016, p. 32). Boundary-spanners, also referred to as knowledge 'brokers' (Contandriopoulos, Lemire, Denis, & Tremblay, 2010, p. 464; Meyer, 2010, p. 118), 'work at the boundaries' (Chau et al., 2017, p. 205) of academia to 'impart tacit as well as codified knowledge to other stakeholders' (Youtie & Shapira, 2008, p. 1202). They carry scientific expertise into various contexts of application, either applying knowledge and solving problems directly, or else transferring or 'brokering' knowledge transactions by taking up roles that 'span' two or more sites of knowledge production, development and application. Boundary-spanners include, for example, those academics who draw on brief spells in industry to generate networks and research agendas in collaboration with users and sponsors; those industry or other non-academic scientists who take on honorary or temporary academic posts in specific collaborative configurations; and those who create academic spin-out companies to patent and commercialise their research-based technologies (Brennan, Papatsiba, Sousa, & Hoffman, 2016). They are of increasing importance to universities and non-academic knowledge-intensive organisations (Henkel, 2004; Hoffman, 2011; Meyer, 2010; Vakkuri, 2004).

Just as important is the boundary-spanning role that students or recent graduates can play. There is much evidence to show that the greatest 'return' from investment in STEMM education and research is the output of human capital in the form of skilled individuals, especially when also trained in research (Coad et al., 2014; Diamond et al., 2014; Frontier Economics, 2014; Hughes & Kitson, 2012; Hughes & Martin, 2012; Pavitt, 1998; Reid, 2014; Salter et al., 2000). That 'students represent an important potential resource' (CERI, 1982, p. 74) for advancing universities' third mission goals has long been acknowledged. The majority of STEMM graduates, even at the PhD level, exit academia and predominantly work in knowledge-intensive areas of scientific application (Royal Society, 2010). This means that academic researchers who are involved in STEMM higher education, particularly the training of doctoral students, are likely to have significant personal connections with individuals in a range of knowledge-intensive organisations who represent potential collaborators, users and even sponsors of academic research. Students 'constitute a bridging component in the establishment, maintenance and expansion of university-industry collaborations' (Ponomariov, 2009, p. 61). For example, Slaughter et al. (2002) find graduate students to be analytically akin to 'tokens of exchange' (p. 305):

> Former students employed by large corporations sometimes continued their involvement with their professors and departments by serving as consulting faculty members and visiting university labs as frequently as

once a week, allowing the former students to keep current on research and identify future employees.... Former students frequently sat on university or college industrial advisory boards and sometimes in that capacity assisted in designing new graduate courses.... When professors wrote proposals to industry, they listed the graduates presently working at the company to show a nondeliverable benefit to the corporation that was valued as highly as any research.

However, the demand for highly skilled (doctoral) graduates also puts new pressures on universities. For example, the increased prominence of boundary-spanning roles of graduates has prompted shifts in higher education curricula, including at doctoral level, towards more 'generic' skills rather than focused solely on disciplinary training (Adkins, 2009; Hancock, Hughes, & Walsh, 2017; Hancock & Walsh, 2014; Henkel, 2004; Mendoza, 2007; Thune, 2010), as students are having 'entrepreneurial' (Papatsiba, 2013, p. 58) identities imposed on them by national and supranational policy agendas. While some see this as an important and legitimate goal of doctoral education given the reality that most doctoral graduates leave academia, critics argue that such 'genericism' could diminish the distinctive scientific value of higher education and, therefore, have a perverse effect on the stock of human knowledge and the criticality and innovativeness of graduates (Beck & Young, 2005; Young, 2008).

The role of boundary-spanners therefore throws up several of the same issues, tensions and dilemmas as the other forms of boundary transaction discussed earlier. It is possible for boundary-spanners to promote synergies across multiple missions and to reinforce academic boundaries while meeting external demands and interests. But they can also cause conflicts, and the importance of addressing these conflicts is heightened when the education and treatment of students is at stake.

Applying the boundary lens

So far, this book has focused primarily on developing conceptual tools for thinking about academia through the lens of the boundary metaphor, grounded in Bernstein's sociological notions of 'power' and 'control' over boundaries and boundary transactions. These conceptual tools help to formulate important questions for empirical research. For example:

- How are academic boundaries and boundary transactions experienced, confronted and crossed by academics?
- Does 'control' over academia's boundary transactions primarily lie with academia or with external actors?

- What role do boundary transactions play in the continuation of or change in academic boundaries?
- How do different institutional or disciplinary contexts mediate interplays of power and control over academic boundaries and boundary transactions?

Chapters 3 and 4 draw from research I conducted addressing such questions. In the remainder of this chapter I will describe key elements of the design for my empirical study in order to show how the principles of the boundary lens can inform and guide empirical research. Additional methodological and sampling details are also provided in the Appendix.

Sampling

I focused my study on cases of United Kingdom-based academic research which the 2014 Research Excellence Framework (REF2014) review process highlighted as highly 'impactful' (see the Appendix for sampling details). The reasoning underpinning this was that it seemed likely that research which had made a significant impact beyond academia would be rich in instances of boundary transactions, and it was essential to my study's aims that I was able to identify and study boundary transactions in their contexts of research.

As discussed in the final section of Chapter 1, I decided to focus on STEMM disciplines. As others have recognised (Hoffman, 2011; Slaughter & Leslie, 1997; Ylijoki, 2003), limiting the epistemic scope of my study in this way allows me to go into detail about the impact of epistemic contexts, while also having sufficient variation across STEMM disciplines to analyse the impacts of (relatively subtle) variations in epistemic context. Within this scope of 'high-impact' STEMM research, I took a 'maximum variation' (Miles & Huberman, 1994, p. 28) approach to sampling, aiming to capture a range of epistemic contexts along two epistemic dimensions: branch of science and research 'orientation' (Hughes et al., 2016, p. 30). Branch of science includes the categories of life sciences, natural sciences and formal sciences. Research 'orientation' refers to whether a discipline is basic, primarily oriented towards the advancement of understanding of phenomena, or applied, oriented primarily towards finding and testing novel applications of knowledge (Stokes, 1997; Ziman, 2005/1994). Table 2.1 details the epistemic characteristics of the ten sampled departments, showing that a good balance of research orientation and branch of science was achieved. Note that the disciplinary groupings align with those used in REF2014. Some disciplinary groupings have characteristics which

Table 2.1 Sampled disciplines and epistemic characteristics

Disciplinary grouping	Epistemic characteristics	
	Research orientation	Branch of science
Clinical Medicine	Applied	Life
Psychology, Psychiatry & Neuroscience	Basic/Applied	Life
Biology	Basic	Life
Earth Systems and Environmental Science	Basic/Applied	Life/Natural
Chemistry	Basic	Natural
Physics	Basic	Natural
Mathematical Sciences	Basic	Formal
Computer Sciences & Informatics	Applied	Formal
Materials & Metallurgy	Applied	Natural/Formal
Civil & Construction Engineering	Applied	Formal
Totals	Basic (6) Applied (6)	Life (4) Natural (4) Formal (4)

fundamentally cross two branches of science and/or which have features of basic and applied research – what I will generally refer to as 'use-inspired basic' disciplines, following Stokes (1997).

I also wanted to explore whether departments with different levels of 'prestige' or 'status' (Boliver, 2015) were able to exert different levels of power and control over boundary transactions. I therefore selected departments associated with different levels of 'prestige', with three classifications: 'elite' (three departments), 'more prestigious' (four departments) and 'less prestigious' (three departments) (see the Appendix for details of how departments were classified).

Data

In order to capture the functioning of boundary transactions, I had to focus the analysis on specific programmes of research. I wanted to capture a similar range and richness of data from each department and, in some cases, this meant studying more than one research project or programme from a department. In total, across the ten departments, I gathered data from 19 distinct programmes of research – between one and three from each department.

The main dataset consisted of 345 documentary and web sources, including:

- information about the research and the department submitted to REF2014;
- outputs from the underpinning research;

- other information about the research such as grant proposals or press releases;
- and any other web pages (mostly institutional) about
  - the research,
  - the individual researchers involved,
  - the units, centres, departments and universities which housed the researchers, and
  - any non-academic actors who emerged as important actors in the research or impact process.

B. R. Clark (1983) referred to academic knowledge as the 'invisible material' (p. 12) upon which the university is grounded. I conceptualise my documentary-led approach to empirical research as an attempt to capture material traces of the invisible material in documents pertaining to its design, purposes, context, production, dissemination and application. However, it is important also to capture the 'personal' (Barry & Slater, 2002, p. 182; Watermeyer, 2011, p. 387, 2016, p. 208) in processes of research and impact generation. I therefore supplemented these documentary materials with ten in-depth interviews with academics who led (or, in one case, did not lead but was closely involved in) the sampled research.

Analysis

While analysing the documentary and interview data, my main aims were to:

1. identify instances of boundary transactions
2. reveal the (potentially simultaneous) role of boundary transactions in
   a. academia enacting its distinctive value(s) and identity (indicating tendencies towards the reproduction of academic boundaries
   b. academia's distinctive value(s) and identities being challenged (indicating tendencies towards the potential weakening of academic boundaries)
3. infer from this whether the boundary transactions associated with the sampled research is leading to the reproduction or the weakening of academic boundaries

Another important part of the analysis was developing an in-depth understanding of the particular contexts in which research-related boundary transactions took place. Boundary transactions do not take place in isolation but in the process of complex, 'multidimensional' (McNie et al. 2016, p. 885) research activities and practices, made all the more complex when academics take interest in the potential use(rs) of their research (Etzkowitz & Viale, 2010; Reed, Bryce, & Machen, 2018; Simon & Schiemer, 2015), as was the case in all of my sampled research.

In order to develop such an in-depth understanding of the programmes of research in my sample, I drew from McNie et al. (2016), who developed a typology which I have found helpful in keeping track of the various and multidimensional ways in which academic research can be more or less oriented towards the weakening or reinforcing of academic boundaries. The authors' original use of the typology was as 'a heuristic' (McNie et al., 2016, p. 893) tool for capturing the ways in which a given research programme or project is oriented either towards the values of the *producers* of scientific knowledge or the *users* of scientific knowledge. With a slight adaptation according to the terminology of my boundary lens, their typology lends itself well as a heuristic tool for analysing the *boundedness* of academic research. By 'the *boundedness* of academic research', I mean that any given instance of academic research has many attributes and activities associated with it, each of which may tend either towards the reinforcing of academic boundaries or towards the opening up and potential weakening of academic boundaries. In my terminology, academic research can be considered relatively 'bounded' if the totality of its associated attributes and activities tend towards the reinforcing of academic boundaries, whereas research whose attributes and activities overall contribute more towards the opening up of boundaries could be considered relatively 'unbounded'. Next, I will briefly describe each of the 15 attributes/activities from McNie et al.'s (2016, pp. 885–890) typology, along with a description of how each attribute/activity might look in the context of 'bounded' and 'unbounded' cases of academic research. Two brief caveats: first, despite my use of extreme descriptors to explain each element of the typology, most real-world research (or at least the research I have studied) is neither extremely 'bounded' nor extremely 'unbounded', but is relatively bounded in some ways and relatively unbounded in others, and the 'boundedness' of research often changes over time. Second, the 15 elements of the typology are not supposed to represent distinctive constituent parts of a thing called 'research'. Rather, the value of the typology is that it highlights the various ways in which, and various angles from which, one may approach the analysis of how academic research engages with and is influenced by the world beyond academic boundaries. In other words, each of these attributes/activities can be of interest in their own right, but a comprehensive understanding of the context in which research is conducted should attempt to bear each of them in mind, as I did in my empirical study.

- The *goals* of research.
  - 'Bounded' research is theoretical, abstract and curiosity-driven, with no preference for what the findings may be other than that they be accurate.
  - 'Unbounded' research is applied, in some extreme cases focused on achieving a narrowly specified real-world outcome, with little interest in advancing knowledge with broader scientific or practical relevance beyond that specific context.
- The *relevance* of research.
  - 'Bounded' research tends to focus only on expanding the generalisability of an academic discipline's knowledge claims.
  - 'Unbounded' research produces knowledge of more localised and direct relevance to a specific user or issue.
- *Evaluation* (or *criteria for success*) of research.
  - 'Bounded' academic research is focused solely on 'internal' criteria, that is, by peer-reviewed assessments of scientific rigour and originality.
  - 'Unbounded' research sees 'success' primarily or exclusively in terms of its 'real-world' impacts, e.g., revenue-generation, improved health outcomes or influence over policy decisions.
- The *outputs and outcomes* of research.
  - 'Bounded' research has the intended outcomes of contributing to a specialist knowledge community via specialist knowledge outputs (such as journal articles).
  - 'Unbounded' research focuses on outputs more likely to lead to real-world outcomes, such as workshops or briefings targeted at nonscientific user communities.
- The approach to *uncertainty*.
  - 'Bounded' research takes pains to hone in on the minutiae of cause-effect relationships and eliminate uncertainty about how the world works.
  - 'Unbounded' research is interested in *what works* rather than *how* things work, and so has no interest in eliminating uncertainty about the world except insofar as that uncertainty prevents us from achieving specific objectives.

- *Knowledge exchange.*
  - 'Bounded' research does not involve any *exchange* – only the transmission of knowledge from academia to 'society' in the form of academic publications.
  - 'Unbounded' research involves learning from the expertise/ experiences of relevant non-academic partners and ensuring that resultant knowledge is meaningful to them.
- *Accessibility.*
  - 'Bounded' research is conducted in 'closed off' organisational contexts which reject external influence.
  - 'Unbounded' research welcomes input and approaches from potential users or stakeholders.
- *Boundary management.*
  - 'Bounded' research aims to avoid boundary management issues by avoiding boundary transactions altogether, or only interacting with 'safe' external actors who present no boundary management issues.
  - 'Unbounded' research enters new kinds of spaces and relationships focused on impact and profit, pushing the 'boundaries' of academic activity and identity and thus regularly facing issues of boundary management.
- *Network participation.*
  - 'Bounded' research is conducted in tightly defined academic networks.
  - 'Unbounded' research involves a wide-reaching and complex network integrating academia with non-academic actors.
- *Flexibility.*
  - 'Bounded' research is unwilling to adapt or shift according to external demands or interests.
  - 'Unbounded' research adapts and changes course according to the needs of user or stakeholder groups.
- *Disciplinary focus.*
  - 'Bounded' research deals with problems, methods and theories which have meaning within a discipline.
  - 'Unbounded' research is not interested in adherence to or contribution to disciplines; disciplines become merely wells of knowledge

or techniques to draw from as the need arises in the context of nondisciplinary objectives.

- Need to mobilise *social capital*.
  - 'Bounded' research perceives no need to develop or mobilise 'social capital', beyond that which may be associated with academic values of expertise, rigour and objectivity, which are the basis of trustworthiness.
  - 'Unbounded' research requires the development and mobilisation of 'social capital', since it is not solely interested in dispassionately transmitting knowledge, but in working collaboratively with a range of stakeholders in order to enact positive change and generate positive impacts.
- *Expertise*.
  - 'Bounded' research is dominated by scientifically trained experts.
  - 'Unbounded' research depends on other forms of expertise as well as scientific, such as political or entrepreneurial expertise.
- The *learning* that results from (what is *learned* from) research.
  - What is learned from 'bounded' research is highly specialised, theoretical and codified knowledge, likely to have meaning primarily only within specialised disciplinary or sub-disciplinary communities.
  - What is learned as a result of 'unbounded' research may be impossible to fully capture in codified forms, since it is (often tacitly) embedded within real-world social contexts and practices within which it is generated.
- The privileging of *human capital*.
  - 'Bounded' research privileges narrowly defined 'human capital', that is, formal scientific training.
  - 'Unbounded' research also greatly values 'softer' skills that have nothing to do with human capital.

In Chapter 3, I present three case studies, selected from my sample of 19 programmes of research. The three case studies serve many purposes, among them being the illustration of how consideration of the 15 attributes/activities can reveal significant differences in the 'boundedness' of different cases of academic research and also reveal the mechanistic role of boundary transactions in crossing, enacting and regulating academic boundaries.

References

Adkins, B. (2009). PhD pedagogy and the changing knowledge landscapes of universities. *Higher Education Research and Development, 28*(2), 165–177. doi:10.1080/07294360902725041

Barry, A., & Born, G. (Eds.). (2013). *Interdisciplinarity: Reconfigurations of the social and natural sciences*. London: Routledge.

Barry, A., Born, G., & Weszkalnys, G. (2008). Logics of interdisciplinarity. *Economy and Society, 37*(1), 20–49. doi:10.1080/03085140701760841

Barry, A., & Slater, D. (2002). Introduction: The technological economy. *Economy and Society, 31*(2), 175–193. doi:10.1080/03085140220123117

Beck, J., & Young, M. (2005). The assault on the professions and the restructuring of academic and professional identities: A Bernsteinian analysis. *British Journal of Sociology of Education, 26*(2), 183–197. doi:10.1080/0142569042000294165

Ben-David, J. (1971). *The scientist's role in society: A comparative study*. Englewood Cliffs: Prentice-Hall.

Ben-David, J. (1977). *Centres of learning: Britain, France, Germany, United States*. New York: McGraw Hill.

Benneworth, P., & Charles, D. (2013). University-community engagement in the wider policy environment. In P. Benneworth (Ed.), *University engagement with socially excluded communities*. Dordrecht: Springer.

Benneworth, P., De Boer, H., & Jongbloed, B. (2015). Between good intentions and urgent stakeholder pressures: Institutionalizing the universities' third mission in the Swedish context. *European Journal of Higher Education, 5*(3), 1–17. doi:10.1080/21568235.2015.1044549

Bernstein, B. (2000). *Pedagogy, symbolic control, and identity: Theory, research, critique* (2nd ed.). Oxford: Rowman & Littlefield.

Bernstein, B. (2003/1990). *Class, codes and control volume IV: The structuring of pedagogic discourse*. London: Routledge.

Bhaskar, R. (2010). Contexts of interdisciplinarity: Interdisciplinarity and climate change. In R. Bhaskar, C. Frank, K. G. Hoyer, P. Næss, & J. Parker (Eds.), *Interdisciplinarity and climate change: Transforming knowledge and practice for our global future*. London: Routledge.

Boliver, V. (2015). Are there distinctive clusters of higher and lower status universities in the UK? *Oxford Review of Education, 41*(5), 608–627. doi:10.1080/03054985.2015.1082905

Brennan, J., Papatsiba, V., Sousa, S. B., & Hoffman, D. (2016). Diversity of higher education institutions in networked knowledge societies: A comparative examination. In D. M. Hoffman & J. Välimaa (Eds.), *Re-becoming universities?: Higher education institutions in networked knowledge societies*. Dordrecht: Springer.

Callon, M. (1994). Is science a public good? *Science, Technology, & Human Values, 19*(4), 395–424. doi:10.1177/016224399401900401

Cantwell, B. (2015). Laboratory management, academic production, and the building blocks of academic capitalism. *Higher Education: The International Journal of Higher Education Research, 70*(3), 487–502. doi:10.1007/s10734-014-9851-9

Cell, J. W. (1982). *The highest stage of White supremacy: The origins of segregation in South Africa and the American South.* Cambridge: Cambridge University Press.

Centre for Educational Research and Innovation. (1982). *The university and the community: The problems of changing relationships.* Paris: Organisation for Economic Co-operation and Development.

Chau, V. S., Gilman, M., & Serbanica, C. (2017). Aligning university–industry interactions: The role of boundary spanning in intellectual capital transfer. *Technological Forecasting & Social Change, 123*(C), 199–209. doi:10.1016/j.techfore.2016.03.013

Clark, B. R. (1983). *The higher education system: Academic organisation in cross-national perspective.* London: University of California Press.

Clark, B. R. (1989). The academic life: Small worlds, different worlds. *Educational Researcher, 18*(5), 4–8. doi:10.3102/0013189X018005004

Clark, B. R. (1995). *Places of inquiry: Research and advanced education in modern universities.* London: University of California Press.

Clark, B. R. (1998). *Creating entrepreneurial universities: Organizational pathways of transformation.* Oxford: Pergamon Press.

Clark, B. R. (2008). Differentiation and integration of the academic profession. In B. R. Clark & A. Clark (Eds.), *On higher education: Selected writings, 1956–2006.* Baltimore: Johns Hopkins University Press.

Clark, W. C., Tomich, T. P., van Noordwijk, M., Guston, D., Catacutan, D., Dickson, N. M., & McNie, E. (2016). Boundary work for sustainable development: Natural resource management at the Consultative Group on International Agricultural Research (CGIAR). *Proceedings of the National Academy of Sciences, 113*(17), 4615. doi:10.1073/pnas.0900231108

Coad, A., Cowlin, M., Nightingale, P., Pellegrino, G., Savona, M., & Siepel, J. (2014). *UK innovation survey: Innovative firms and growth.* Retrieved from https://assets.publishing.service.gov.uk/government/uploads/system/uploads/attachment_data/file/289234/bis-14-643-uk-innovation-survey-highly-innovative-firms-and-growth.pdf

Contandriopoulos, D., Lemire, M., Denis, J. L., & Tremblay, E. (2010). Knowledge exchange processes in organizations and policy arenas: A narrative systematic review of the literature. *Milbank Quarterly, 88*(4), 444–483. doi:10.1111/j.1468-0009.2010.00608.x

Diamond, A., Ball, C., Vorley, T., Hughes, T., Moreton, R., Howe, P., & Nathwani, T. (2014). *Impact of doctoral careers.* Retrieved from www.rcuk.ac.uk/publications/reports/impact-of-doctoral-careers/

Durkheim, É. (2013). *The evolution of educational thought: Lectures on the formation and development of secondary education in France.* Oxon: Routledge.

Etzkowitz, H. (2008). *The triple helix: University-industry-government innovation in action.* New York: Routledge.

Etzkowitz, H., & Leydesdorff, L. (1995). The triple helix – University-industry-government relations: A laboratory for knowledge based economic development. *EASST Review, 14*(1), 14–19. doi:10.1007%2F978-1-4614-3858-8_452

Etzkowitz, H., & Viale, R. (2010). Polyvalent knowledge and the entrepreneurial university: A third academic revolution? *Critical Sociology*, *36*(4), 595–609. doi:10.1177/0896920510365921

Frontier Economics. (2014). *Rates of return to investment in science and innovation: A report prepared for the Department for Business Innovation and Skills (BIS)*. Retrieved from https://assets.publishing.service.gov.uk/government/uploads/system/uploads/attachment_data/file/333006/bis-14-990-rates-of-return-to-investment-in-science-and-innovation-revised-final-report.pdf

Gibbons, M., Limoges, C., Nowotny, H., Schwartzman, S., Scott, P., & Trow, M. (1994). *The new production of knowledge: The dynamics of science and research in contemporary societies*. London: Sage.

Guston, D. H. (1999). Stabilizing the boundary between US politics and science: The role of the office of technology transfer as a boundary organization. *Social Studies of Science*, *29*(1), 87–111. doi:10.1177/030631299029001004

Hancock, S., Hughes, G., & Walsh, E. (2017). Purist or pragmatist? UK doctoral scientists' moral positions on the knowledge economy. *Studies in Higher Education*, *42*(7), 1244–1258. doi:10.1080/03075079.2015.1087994

Hancock, S., & Walsh, E. (2014). Beyond knowledge and skills: Rethinking the development of professional identity during the STEM doctorate. *Studies in Higher Education*, *5079* (February 2015), 1–14. doi:10.1080/03075079.2014.915301

Henkel, M. (2004). Current science policies and their implications for the formation and maintenance of academic identity. *Higher Education Policy*, *17*(2), 167. doi:10.1057/palgrave.hep.8300049

Hoffman, S. G. (2011). The new tools of the science trade: Contested knowledge production and the conceptual vocabularies of academic capitalism. *Social Anthropology*, *19*(4), 439–462. doi:10.1111/j.1469-8676.2011.00180.x

Hughes, A., & Kitson, M. (2012). Pathways to impact and the strategic role of universities: New evidence on the breadth and depth of university knowledge exchange in the UK and the factors constraining its development. *Cambridge Journal of Economics*, *36*(3), 723–750. doi:10.1093/cje/bes017

Hughes, A., Lawson, C., Kitson, M., Salter, A., Bullock, A., & Hughes, R. B. (2016). *The changing state of knowledge exchange: UK academic interactions with external organisations 2005–2015*. Retrieved from www.ncub.co.uk/reports/national-survey-of-academics.html

Hughes, A., & Martin, B. (2012). *Enhancing impact: The value of public sector R&D*. Retrieved from www.ncub.co.uk/impact

Jongbloed, B., Enders, J., & Salerno, C. (2008). Higher education and its communities: Interconnections, interdependencies and a research agenda. *The International Journal of Higher Education and Educational Planning*, *56*(3), 303–324. doi:10.1007/s10734-008-9128-2

Kaidesoja, T., & Kauppinen, I. (2014). How to explain academic capitalism: A mechanism-based approach. In B. Cantwell & I. Kauppinen (Eds.), *Academic capitalism in the age of globalization*. Baltimore: Johns Hopkins University Press.

Kantasalmi, K., & Tuunainen, J. (2018). Discipline-making and organizational permeability of the university: Discussing the notion of organizational field. *Research in the Sociology of Organizations, 57*, 331–359. doi:10.1108/S0733-558X20180000057013

Knorr-Cetina, K. D. (1983). The ethnographic study of scientific work: Towards a constructivist interpretation of science. In K. D. Knorr-Cetina & M. J. Mulkay (Eds.), *Science observed: Perspectives on the social study of science*. London: Sage.

Krishnan, A. (2009). *What are academic disciplines? Some observations on the disciplinarity vs. interdisciplinary debate*. Working Paper. Retrieved from http://eprints.ncrm.ac.uk/783/

Lähteenmäki-Smith, K. (2014). Implementing innovation policy. In K. Halme, I. Lindy, K. A. Piirainen, V. Salminen, & J. White (Eds.), *Finland as a knowledge economy 2.0: Lessons on policies and governance*. Washington, DC: The World Bank.

Lam, A. (2007). Knowledge networks and careers: Academic scientists in industry – University links. *Journal of Management Studies, 44*(6), 993–1016. doi:10.1111/j.1467-6486.2007.00696.x

Lam, A. (2015). Shifting institutional boundaries: 'Boundary work' of academic scientists in the entrepreneurial university. In E. Reale & E. Primeri (Eds.), *The transformation of university institutional and organizational boundaries* (pp. 1–28). Rotterdam: Sense.

Leydesdorff, L., & Etzkowitz, H. (2001). The transformation of university-industry-government relations. *Electronic Journal of Sociology, 5*(4).

McNie, E. C., Parris, A., & Sarewitz, D. (2016). Improving the public value of science: A typology to inform discussion, design and implementation of research. *Research Policy, 45*(4), 884–895. doi:10.1016/j.respol.2016.01.004

Mendoza, P. (2007). Academic capitalism and doctoral student socialization: A case study. *The Journal of Higher Education, 78*(1), 71–96. doi:10.1080/00221546.2007.11778964

Meyer, M. (2010). The rise of the knowledge broker. *Science Communication, 32*(1), 118–127. doi:10.1177/1075547009359797

Miles, M. B., & Huberman, M. A. (1994). *Qualitative data analysis: An expanded sourcebook* (2nd ed.). London: Sage.

Moore, R. (2013). *Basil Bernstein: The thinker and the field*. London: Routledge.

Morgan Jones, M., Manville, C., & Chataway, J. (2017). Learning from the UK's research impact assessment exercise: A case study of a retrospective impact assessment exercise and questions for the future. *Journal of Technology Transfer*, 1–25. doi:10.1007/s10961-017-9608-6

Muellerleile, C., & Lewis, N. (2019). Re-assembling knowledge production with(out) the university. *Globalisation, Societies and Education, 17*(1), 1–10. doi:10.1080/14767724.2019.1602352

Nickolai, D. H., Hoffman, S. G., & Trautner, M. N. (2012). Can a knowledge sanctuary also be an economic engine? The marketization of higher education as institutional boundary work. *Sociology Compass, 6*(3), 205–218. doi:10.1111/j.1751-9020.2011.00449.x

North, D. C. (1990). *Institutions, institutional change and economic performance*. Cambridge: Cambridge University Press.

Nowotny, H. (2005). The increase of complexity and its reduction. *Theory, Culture & Society, 22*(5), 15–31. doi:10.1177/0263276405057189

Nowotny, H. (2006). *The potential of transdisciplinarity*. Retrieved from www.helga-nowotny.eu/downloads/helga_nowotny_b59.pdf

Nowotny, H., Scott, P., & Gibbons, M. (2003). Introduction: 'Mode 2' revisited: The new production of knowledge. *Minerva, 41*(3), 179–194. doi:10.1023/A%3A1025505528250

Nyhagen, G., & Baschung, L. (2013). New organisational structures and the transformation of academic work. *Higher Education, 66*(4), 409–423. doi:10.1007/s10734-013-9612-1

Olssen, M. (2011). The strange death of the liberal university: Research assessments and the impact of research. In *Handbook on globalization and higher education* (pp. 360–383). Cheltenham: Edward Elgar Publishing.

Papatsiba, V. (2013). Policy goals of European integration and competitiveness in academic collaborations: An examination of Joint Master's and Erasmus Mundus Programmes. *Higher Education Policy, 27*(1), 43–64. doi:10.1057/hep.2013.13

Pavitt, K. (1998). The social shaping of the national science base. *Research Policy, 27*(8), 793–805. doi:10.1016/S0048-7333(98)00091-2

Perkin, H. (1984). The historical perspective. In B. R. Clark (Ed.), *Perspectives on higher education: Eight disciplinary and comparative views*. London: University of California Press.

Petersen, A. M., Rotolo, D., & Leydesdorff, L. (2016). A triple helix model of medical innovation: Supply, demand, and technological capabilities in terms of Medical Subject Headings. *Research Policy, 45*(3), 666–681. doi:10.1016/j.respol.2015.12.004

Polanyi, M. (1962). Tacit knowing. *Philosophy Today, 6*(4), 239. doi:10.5840/philtoday19626427

Polanyi, M. (1998). *Personal knowledge: Towards a post-critical philosophy*. London: Taylor & Francis.

Ponomariov, B. (2009). Student centrality in university–industry interactions. *Industry and Higher Education, 23*(1), 50–62. doi:10.1630/0326785041834748

Ponomariov, B., & Boardman, C. (2010). Influencing scientists' collaboration and productivity patterns through new institutions: University research centers and scientific and technical human capital. *Research Policy, 39*(5), 613–624. doi:10.1016/j.respol.2010.02.013

Reed, M., Bryce, R., & Machen, R. (2018). Pathways to policy impact: A new approach for planning and evidencing research impact. *Evidence & Policy: A Journal of Research, Debate and Practice, 14*(3), 431–458. doi:10.1332/174426418X15326967547242

Reid, G. (2014). *Why should the taxpayer fund science & research?* National Centre for University and Business. Retrieved from https://www.ncub.co.uk/reports/why-science.html

Royal Society. (2010). *The scientific century: Securing our future prosperity*. Retrieved from https://royalsociety.org/~/media/Royal_Society_Content/policy/publications/2010/4294970126.pdf

Salter, A., D'Este, P., Martin, B., Geuna, A., Scott, A., Pavitt, K., Nightingale, P., & Patel, P. (2000). *Talent, not technology: Publicly funded research and innovation in the UK*. London: CVCP.

Sataøen, H. L. (2018). Transforming the "third mission" in Norwegian higher education institutions: A boundary object theory approach. *Scandinavian Journal of Educational Research*, *62*(1), 52–67. doi:10.1080/00313831.2016.1212253

Simon, D., & Schiemer, F. (2015). Crossing boundaries: Complex systems, transdisciplinarity and applied impact agendas. *Current Opinion in Environmental Sustainability*, *12*, 6–11. doi:10.1016/j.cosust.2014.08.007

Slaughter, S., Archerd, C. J., & Campbell, T. I. D. (2004). Boundaries and quandaries: How professors negotiate market relations. *Review of Higher Education*, *28*(1), 129–165. doi:10.1353/rhe.2004.0032

Slaughter, S., Campbell, T., Holleman, M., & Morgan, E. (2002). The "traffic" in graduate students: Graduate students as tokens of exchange between academe and industry. *Science, Technology, & Human Values*, *27*(2), 282–312. doi:10.1177/016224390202700205

Slaughter, S., & Leslie, L. L. (1997). *Academic capitalism: Politics, policies, and the entrepreneurial university*. London: Johns Hopkins University Press.

Slaughter, S., & Rhoades, G. (2010). *Academic capitalism and the new economy: Markets, state, and higher education*. Baltimore, MD: Johns Hopkins University Press.

Smith, S., Ward, V., & House, A. (2011). 'Impact' in the proposals for the UK's Research Excellence Framework: Shifting the boundaries of academic autonomy. *Research Policy*, *40*(10), 1369–1379. doi:10.1016/j.respol.2011.05.026

Sousa-Ginel, E., Franco-Leal, N., & Camelo-Ordaz, C. (2017). The influence of networks on the knowledge conversion capability of academic spin-offs. *Industrial and Corporate Change*, *26*(6), 1125–1144. doi:10.1093/icc/dtx013

Star, S. L., & Griesemer, J. R. (1989). Institutional ecology, 'translations' and boundary objects: Amateurs and professionals in Berkeley's Museum of Vertebrate Zoology, 1907–39. *Social Studies of Science*, *19*(3), 387–420. doi:10.1177/030631289019003001

Stokes, D. E. (1997). *Pasteur's quadrant: Basic science and technological innovation*. Washington, DC: Brookings Institution Press.

Taheri, M., & van Geenhuizen, M. (2016). Teams' boundary-spanning capacity at university: Performance of technology projects in commercialization. *Technological Forecasting & Social Change*, *111*, 31–43. doi:10.1016/j.techfore.2016.06.003

Thune, T. (2010). The training of "triple helix workers"? Doctoral students in university-industry-government collaborations. *Minerva: A Review of Science, Learning and Policy*, *48*(4), 463–483. doi:10.1007/s11024-010-9158-7

Tilly, C. (1998). *Durable inequality*. Berkeley, CA: University of California Press.

Vakkuri, J. (2004). Institutional change of universities as a problem of evolving boundaries. *Higher Education Policy*, *17*(3), 287–309. doi:10.1057/palgrave.hep.8300056

Variainen, P., & Viiri, A. (2005). Universities and their local partners: The case of the University of Joensuu. In A. Antikainen (Ed.), *Transforming a learning society: The case of Finland*. Oxford: Peter Lang.

Watermeyer, R. (2011). Challenges for university engagement in the UK: Towards a public academe? *Higher Education Quarterly*, *65*(4), 386–410. doi:10.1111/j.1468-2273.2011.00492.x

Watermeyer, R. (2016). Impact in the REF: Issues and obstacles. *Studies in Higher Education*, *41*(2), 199–214. doi:10.1080/03075079.2014.915303

Watermeyer, R., & Olssen, M. (2016). 'Excellence' and exclusion: The individual costs of institutional competitiveness. *A Review of Science, Learning and Policy*, *54*(2), 201–218. doi:10.1007/s11024-016-9298-5

Ylijoki, O.-H. (2003). Entangled in academic capitalism? A case-study on changing ideals and practices of university research. *Higher Education*, *45*(3), 307–335. doi:10.1023/A:1022667923715

Young, M. (2008). *Bringing knowledge back in: From social constructivism to social realism in the sociology of education*. London: Routledge.

Youtie, J., & Shapira, P. (2008). Building an innovation hub: A case study of the transformation of university roles in regional technological and economic development. *Research Policy*, *37*(8), 1188–1204. doi:10.1016/j.respol.2008.04.012

Ziman, J. M. (1996). Postacademic science: Constructing knowledge with networks and norms. *Science Studies*, *9*(1), 67–80.

Ziman, J. M. (2005/1994). *Prometheus bound: Science in a dynamic steady state*. Cambridge: Cambridge University Press.

Zomer, A., & Benneworth, P. (2011). The rise of the university's third mission. In J. Enders, H. F. de Boer, & D. F. Westerheijden (Eds.), *Reform of higher education in Europe* (pp. 81–101). Rotterdam: Sense.

3 Zoom in
STEMM research through the boundary lens

I have argued that the long-term reproduction of academic boundaries depends in large part on engaging in (potentially costly) boundary transactions which contribute to society, but doing so in a controlled or regulated way, such that boundary transactions serve as a mechanism for enacting rather than undermining academic values and identities. This calls for empirical analyses of the functioning and effects of boundary transactions. In the first section of this chapter, I present three case studies focusing on the enactment and role of boundary transactions in three different programmes of research, selected from my larger sample of 19 programmes of research. In the second section of this chapter, I shift focus to 'zoom in' on each of the five forms of boundary transaction individually. Taking each in turn, I analyse how boundary transactions can function as mechanisms through which academia is able to regulate its boundary relations and reinforce or even enhance its position in society, using both specific examples and aggregate-level data related to the use of and effects of each form of boundary transaction.

Case study analysis of boundary transactions in context

These illustrative case studies go into depth about the programmes of research and the role of boundary transactions within them. I deliberately chose illustrative case studies which varied in their overall level of 'boundedness':

- the first case displays academia in a relatively open and 'unbounded' mode, where academic boundaries appear to be relatively weakly regulated and control over boundary transactions relatively low;
- the second case displays academia in a relatively closed and 'bounded' mode, reproducing and more tightly regulating its boundaries, also exerting greater control over the form of boundary transactions;

- the third case is chosen as an example of one falling somewhere in between the two more extreme cases.

For each case, I will provide a brief narrative of the programme of research, highlighting key boundary transactions and major developments as well as reflect on the 'boundedness' of each case.

Case 1. Unbounded research

The first case is from the field of computer science and informatics and is based within an academic research centre – I will refer to it simply as the Informatics Research Centre. The Centre is a form of 'boundary structure' (according to definitions provided earlier). It aims to bring together multi-disciplinary academics and non-academic experts.

The background and setting for this programme of research is hospitals, going back to the 1980s when there emerged a policy interest in better understanding how surgical practices and outcomes compared across hospitals. This created a demand for research into the factors likely to affect surgical outcomes, so that they could be accounted for in benchmarking and standardisation. For example, any benchmarking tool had to be able to account for the fact that negative surgical outcomes are not just a factor of the individual hospital or surgeon but are also dependent on patient characteristics such as age and medical history.

Some such audit systems did already exist. However, a collaborative team of researchers which brought together medical doctors, medical physicists and statisticians from the Informatics Research Centre and a local NHS Trust identified significant limitations in existing audit systems. This team was therefore motivated to conduct new and more systematic data collection and statistical refinement in order to improve the reliability of existing systems' formula and predictive capabilities.

The Centre consolidated their relations with the NHS Trust through the appointment of one NHS medical physicist as a professor at the Centre. This 'boundary-spanner' became a key link between the Centre and the Trust as they advanced the research in two distinct but interrelated directions over the following decade into the early 2000s. First, the research team broadened its scope by applying its new model to general medicine cases rather than only to surgery outcomes. Second, beyond being just a benchmarking and comparison tool, it targeted direct real-time application in clinical contexts. The aim was to produce an algorithm based on routinely collected patient data, including biographical data and vital signs data, that would generate an Early Warning Score which would identify and rank in real time those patients most at risk of immediate deterioration and therefore in need of extra monitoring and care.

To make this scalable throughout an entire hospital or NHS Trust, it was necessary to reach out ('outreach') to two new kinds of partner. The first, starting in the mid-2000s, was with private sector specialists in medical informatics. This partnership centred around developing a commercial product to digitise the process of gathering and disseminating data to hospital staff in real time. The second involved engaging with medical professional bodies whose support was important in adoption of the system across the NHS.

This programme of research has, then, been driven far more by the policy demand for benchmarking tools and the more fundamental demand for improved health care and outcomes than by any single academic discipline. This is reflected in the research aims; the researchers did not aim to fully solve the complex scientific question of what causes deterioration in different types of patients – which would require significant amounts of data collection and controlling of multiple variables. Rather, they took a more pragmatic and epistemically more modest approach to informing clinical practice by aiming to find ways of using inpatient data that is already routinely collected by hospitals to provide approximate predictions of inpatient deterioration and inform clinical practitioners' priorities.

This is not to say that the research should be considered *non*-academic, nor by any means fully unbounded from academic and scientific norms and systems. Indeed, a significant part of the many-year process was gaining credibility through traditional channels of peer-reviewed academic journal articles. Moreover, almost all actors involved in the research, regardless of whether they were based in universities or not, were united by holding doctorates, the cornerstone of academic credibility and identity, and the basis of an 'epistemic community' (McNie, Parris, & Sarewitz, 2016, p. 889).

However, what stood out in this research programme compared to many of the others sampled was that such academic outputs as journal articles, and such academic expertise as displayed by the doctorate, although necessary, were far from sufficient. The research team would not have been able to advance its research in the necessary way if it were not for other forms of non-academic expertise and skills, such as practical clinical experience, technological skills and entrepreneurship. From the earliest stages, the codified knowledge associated with academic outputs would have been irrelevant if not also for the 'practical' elements of learning which involved 'changing behaviour' of a wide range of hospital staff (McNie et al., 2016, p. 888).

Moreover, as the research progressed, the academic members of the research team engaged in more explicit boundary-crossing activities such as 'outreach' to leverage support for the uptake of research and even became market actors through generating a for-profit start-up company (a highly *unbounded* form of 'boundary structure'). More effort was being expended on 'boundary management', 'network participation' and mobilising 'social capital' in order to achieve their ambitions of commercialisation and policy influence (McNie et al., 2016), and less was being focused on publishing and fine-tuning the model. The outputs are increasingly 'user-oriented', taking the form of patents and other forms of codified knowledge, such as toolkits and technologies. At a certain point, what publishing did take place was not so much reports of new and improved capabilities of the model, but more about showing how the model compared in practice with competitors, while the timely dissemination of knowledge came up against commercial confidentiality.

All five of the different forms of 'boundary transaction' played a part in this programme of research. The Centre is itself an example of a 'boundary structure'. It engaged in significant 'outreach', first as part of building a research 'collaboration' team with NHS Trust scientists and medical practitioners, and later with wider policy and sector bodies and technology entrepreneurs, and this collaboration manifested in co-authored journal articles. At least one key 'boundary-spanner', appointed to a professorship from his previous research post within the NHS, was one of the main driving forces underpinning the research team's initial studies and then later success in leveraging support from external stakeholders. There were also several 'user-oriented outputs' of the research, most obviously the commercial device which digitised and streamlined application of the research team's model, but also in the form of journal articles targeting practitioner audiences. Significantly, several of the academics involved took co-ownership over the company which went on to finalise the development, promotion and marketing of the product. Although underpinned by academic research and specialised scientific knowledge content, the focus on developing, marketing and commercialising a product for private profit which characterised much of the research meant that its strategies, relationships and dissemination practices – in short, its boundary transactions – appeared similar to what would be expected of a small, knowledge-intensive business.

Case 2. *Moderately bounded research*

The second case is from biology. The relevant research centre, which I will call the Marine Research Unit, had a focus on the sub-field of marine ecology. The Unit in fact started life in the 1970s as a non-academic public research unit within the Natural Environment Research Council (NERC), created to fulfil NERC's obligation to advise the UK Government on ecological management, and only became part of a university in 1996, although it still receives NERC funding to continue fulfilment of NERC's obligations. The Marine Research Unit can be conceptualised as a boundary structure which brings together a 'transdisciplinary' (McNie et al., 2016, p. 888) group of experts, including ecologists, zoologists, statisticians and engineers.

This programme of research commenced in the 1990s and focused on the behaviour of predators in marine ecosystems, with the key social need for such knowledge being that marine predators are at risk from humans since they are in competition with human fisheries for fish, prompting calls from fisheries to control populations of predators. Sustainable control requires detailed knowledge about both population distribution and behaviour, particularly behaviour related to foraging habits. Therefore, driven by the desire to inform economic, environmental and political debate around population management, research at the Marine Research Unit was focused on improving instrumentation for remotely tracking and collecting data about marine predators in their natural habitats, as well as on statistical research and innovations which would be able to cope with the highly complex data that was now being collected. Once developed, the Unit then also began to explore, develop and explain how their technological, methodological and theoretical advances had potentially broader applications in conservation management, as well as for those sectors potentially affected by conservation regulations, such as the energy and naval industries, whose operations often bring them into contact with marine life.

This research programme, and the Unit more generally, exhibit interesting boundary relations. On the one hand, the Unit exhibits characteristics of a transdisciplinary boundary structure, whose integration is 'organised around problems' (McNie et al., 2016, p. 888) generated beyond academia. That is, it is oriented towards informing the real-life context of marine life and its interaction with human society, and the political dynamics this creates vis-à-vis tensions between economic activity and ecological conservation. On the other hand, this integration of scientific expertise and the approach and content of the research is 'largely guided by ... disciplines' (McNie et al., 2016, p. 887), specifically the sub-discipline of mammalogy, and the research objectives are framed within and guided by this disciplinary context.

As the research and related activities became more outward-focused, the Unit exhibited three main approaches to boundary transactions, but in each case, they were able to maintain control over the form of their boundary transactions such that they served to reinforce rather than undermine their distinctive academic identities and values whilst simultaneously contributing to relevant practice and policy contexts. First, rather than abandon the preferred form of disseminating knowledge, namely academic journals, one of the main ways in which they informed a wide range of actors close to conservation management practice was precisely through their publishing activities, albeit doing so with a subtle but important change in approach. That is, rather than publishing in marine ecology specific journals, as had normally been the case in the past, they started publishing in more general ecology journals, so that they could publish their research-informed good practices to a wider audience without incurring any notable boundary transaction costs (with the only conceivable 'cost' being the opportunity cost of not publishing in a more specialist journal). Second, the Unit's academics often engaged in outreach events aimed at providing relevant knowledge and training to professionals related to conservation policy or practice. Such cases were perceived by the academics to be very much enactments of their sense of a publicly engaged academic identity, since they perceived themselves to be engaging in this outreach for the good of policy and practice, sometimes doing so without consultancy fees or any other immediate benefit to themselves or their departments. Lastly, the Unit promoted uptake of their technologies sold via an academic spin-out company. However, all the company's profits are put back into funding the Unit's research activity, so that the boundary transaction is in service to academic missions.

With the benefit of insights from McNie et al.'s (2016) framework, there are two particularly interesting factors that emerged as shaping the Marine Research Unit's approach to boundary transactions and boundary regulation. First, it is precisely because of the politically and economically contested nature of ecological conservation issues that the Unit was so keen to maintain a strong academic identity in their boundary transactions. Although 'soft skills' associated with 'communication, translation and mediation' were important, these are secondary to the 'credibility' associated with the 'specific training, norms and behaviours . . . consistent with those in academia' and which lead to academics 'being considered experts in their field and . . . by society' (McNie et al., 2016, pp. 887, 890). Their academic identity therefore lowered the 'risk of politicization' of their work (McNie et al., 2016 p. 890).

Second, at the same time as facing external boundary pressures to cross boundaries and engage with non-academic actors, the Unit was also experiencing significant internal boundary pressures pushing in the opposite direction. Since shifting identity as a public research unit within NERC to an academic research unit, the Unit has had to establish its internal legitimacy amidst some critique about whether it was sufficiently 'academic'. One of my interviewees told of how the Unit felt the need to overcome this non-academic identity in the eyes of their new academic peers, forcing them to consciously limit their boundary-crossing and to ensure they remain focused also on more traditional departmental activities, such as building a strong student base and publishing in disciplinary journals. The interviewee also expressed the need for caution about engaging with certain kinds of stakeholders or users, since it was perceived that research or consultancy sponsored by groups with commercial interests in the results could be considered illegitimate.

To summarise, the Marine Research Unit is a boundary structure, what I term a 'transdisciplinary' boundary structure, in that it brings together biologists, physicists, statisticians and technologists whose expertise coalesces around the sub-field of marine mammalogy. It also has its own offshoot boundary structures in the form of spin-outs which aim to generate consultancy and technology sales revenue. More than just a boundary structure, the Unit can be conceptualised as a 'boundary-*spanning* structure', since for two decades it existed as a non-academic public research institute conducting scientific research directly for policy and regulatory purposes. It now continues these functions, but it does so through its boundary transactions such as 'outreach' and 'user-oriented outputs', such as technologies, workshops, advice and consultancy, as well as journal articles targeting broad audiences. The Unit is careful to uphold a strict, 'bounded' notion of academic identity in its transactions. Overall then, the boundary transactions associated with this research programme reinforced the distinctive value, legitimacy and identity of academia and thereby functioned towards the reproduction of academic boundaries, largely by (i) working within a particular kind of (use-inspired basic) disciplinary context such that the contribution to 'impactful' knowledge was inseparable from their contribution to 'basic' scientific knowledge, and (ii) placing great reliance on their academic and scientific capital as the basis for legitimacy in informing policy debates and decision making.

Case 3. Bounded research

The third and final illustrative case sits within the inherently interdisciplinary and use-inspired field of psychopharmacology, which is concerned with the effect of pharmaceuticals on cognitive functioning. The research was conducted by what I will call the Psychopharmacology Research Group. Within this disciplinary context, the main guiding principle for the Group's research agenda has been delineating the extent of long-term health impacts of exposure to certain drugs in order to inform the health profession, drug users and government policy.

In this case, the drug in question was MDMA, popularly known as 'ecstasy'. In the 1990s, there were reports that MDMA could have certain benefits to the user, and some suggestions that these could potentially outweigh the known risks. The research interests of the Psychopharmacology Research Group could therefore be summarised under two main questions: *Do the negative effects of MDMA outweigh apparent benefits? What psychopharmacological mechanisms underpin observed effects?* The Group conducted systematic reviews and novel empirical studies which analysed, in greater detail than previous work, the negative effects of MDMA on cognitive functioning and mood in both the short and long term. Moreover, the research showed that the strength of these effects correlate with both frequency and quantity of MDMA use. Additionally, in terms of the underpinning scientific mechanisms, the Group provided strong evidence in support of the hypothesis that these effects are the direct result of damage to neurons which release a chemical (serotonin) that is associated both with the feeling of elation brought on by ecstasy pills and with cognitive functioning (e.g., memory).

With the first phase of research having scientifically demonstrated the negative effects of MDMA more vividly and strongly than previous findings, the Group conducted follow-up work focused more on the real-life contexts of MDMA use and its impacts. Specifically, this second stage of research investigated the extent, nature and mediating factors (i.e., frequency, length and conditions of MDMA use) of negative effects in users. Their findings, including the more severe and longer-term effects of prolonged use, directly influenced UK governmental policy around MDMA's classification status.

This work also contributed to raised awareness and the emergence of concerns about the effects that MDMA use by pregnant women may have on children after birth, in turn prompting a new phase of the research which involved a large-scale, longitudinal study. This issue became a somewhat popular topic in the media and with the public, leading to Psychopharmacology Research Groups academics' involvement in more public forms of engagement, such as talks and interviews via international media, governmental agencies and pregnancy and parenting websites, as well as with medical professionals.

Overall, despite these latter instances of 'outreach', I found this to be a very 'bounded' programme of research. Throughout, 'epistemic' expertise and the highest levels of academically bestowed 'human capital' (McNie et al., 2016, pp. 887, 890) were the criteria for engagement in the research, with all involved having PhDs and academic research posts, and with the research predominantly focused on 'understanding [psychopharmacological] theories and . . . [generating] explicit knowledge' (McNie et al., 2016, p. 888). Unlike the other two case studies, there was no stage of the research at which the main focus shifted to development or dissemination – each discernible stage was focused on addressing disciplinary-grounded, empirical research questions, and the main site of evaluation was that of scientific opinion by peer review. Any knowledge exchange that took place was effectively only the 'one-way' (McNie et al., 2016, p. 888) communication of science to society through journal articles, which, in this case, was targeted at a specialist audience, and occasionally advice to government officials, medical professionals and the public. There was therefore little if any need for 'social capital', 'boundary management' or 'flexibility' to evolving external issues, apart from responding to opportunities for advancing the research. This does not, of course, imply that the Group was not cognizant of or interested in the real-world impacts of their research. It simply means that the way in which this interest manifested was heavily mediated by the strong 'disciplinary focus' of their research (McNie et al., 2016, p. 888); the Group's most effective route to impact lay in working within the boundaries of the use-inspired interdisciplinary sub-field of psychopharmacology.

This programme of research primarily exhibits three of the five main forms of boundary transaction: 'boundary structures', 'user-oriented outputs' and 'outreach'. The Group 'reaches out' to policymakers and health practitioners, as well as to the public via various media platforms with specific research findings. One of the relevant concepts that they use is that of 'serotonin syndrome', which functions as what I call a 'bridging concept' (a form of 'user-oriented output'). A 'bridging concept' condenses underpinning scientific research and theory into a more readily understandable concept so as to be suitable for consideration and application by non-specialist users and stakeholders. The bridging concept in this case, 'serotonin syndrome', refers to negative effects associated with given levels of chemical build-up of serotonin caused by using MDMA. The Group's research using this concept has fed into MDMA policy as described earlier, and the concept itself is referred to on NHS webpages aimed at the general public, so that in this case the concept has also 'bridged' to the public domain.

What this case highlights, then, is that research which is strongly science-oriented and operates primarily within the confines of academic boundaries can, at least under certain conditions, be conducive to highly effective boundary-crossing transactions which go on to have 'significant impact' (as judged by REF2014).

The five forms of transaction as boundary-regulating mechanisms

In the second section of this chapter, I shift focus to analyse how each of the five forms of boundary transaction can function as a mechanism through which academia is able to regulate its boundary relations and reinforce or even enhance its position in society. Of course, in reality, there are often multiple forms of boundary transaction operating within the contexts of research and related activity, sometimes simultaneously, with complex implications for academic boundaries, as discussed in the case studies previously. The purpose of this section is therefore to get a better handle on the complex interactions shaping and reshaping academia's role in society by abstracting each form of boundary transaction and considering it in relative isolation, albeit with the knowledge that the precise way in which any boundary transaction operates will be highly context-dependent. Also, although I show how each mechanism achieves this in slightly different ways and to slightly different extents, I want to stress that these differences are not as important as my broader point. Namely, that all forms of transaction *can*, and in many cases *do*, function to reinforce academic boundaries even though, at face value, the fact of crossing boundaries appears to risk undermining and potentially weakening these boundaries.

There are a couple of key indicators that I will look for when highlighting this role for boundary transactions. The first is where boundary transactions provide academics with opportunities to enact their academic identities whilst simultaneously delivering some value to non-academic actors. This serves to reinforce and re-legitimate academia's boundedness (i.e., its distinctiveness and autonomy) by showing the wider societal value of tolerating and maintaining this boundedness. The second is where boundary transactions, which are, on the face of it, activities primarily oriented towards the third mission of societal benefit and 'impact', simultaneously provide academics with opportunities to advance their other core missions of research and teaching/training. This is an indicator of academics exerting control over their boundary transactions and not being pressured towards transactions that are less likely to have any relevance to academia's traditional core missions.

1. Outreach

My analysis finds that, for the most part, outreach is a relatively 'light touch' form of boundary transaction. Outreach does not entail the kinds of intensive interactions associated with the other forms of boundary transaction, as will become clear as I discuss the other transactions. This means two things. Firstly, outreach activities tend to be less 'costly' and risky, since they are less likely to put academics in situations where their distinctive academic identities or values may be challenged or undermined. Second, and for the same reason, outreach can be more limiting in its ability to provide academics with opportunities to enact their distinctive academic identities and to advance other academic missions. However, even outreach can occasionally serve these functions. For example, Figure 3.1 shows that in nearly half

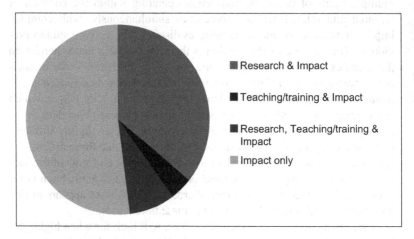

Figure 3.1 Pie chart showing outreach activities contributing to different missions

of all cases of outreach, some core academic mission, normally research but occasionally teaching/training, was advanced alongside the third mission. While this indicates a lower proportion than other forms of transaction, it is still significant.

Interestingly, and prefiguring part of the discussion of future chapters, the data suggests that one of the factors influencing the opportunities that outreach may offer for academics to advance their core missions is the type of external recipient or beneficiary of outreach. For example, when recipients of outreach were policy actors, as was common, there appeared little opportunity for core activities to be advanced. Indeed, I only found one such case. In this case, ecological scientists conducted outreach targeting national and local governmental organisations in various countries to offer expert advice but also, more than that, to seek the political (and, less importantly, some financial) support for their project, which combined novel conservation management techniques with academic research. The same project was also one of the few to engage members of the public, as local communities would collaborate on and directly benefit from the conservation project, and was the only one in which this public engagement was fundamentally intertwined with the research itself and not just the research impact.

Another common group of recipients of outreach were professional practitioners, such as health professionals and scientists in non-academic contexts, such as public bodies or industry. Such outreach seems to offer greater opportunities for advancing core missions than policy outreach. For example, in one case, specialist heart failure nurses who were initially intended to be the recipients of outreach ended up using their own expertise to generate valuable research data that other kinds of professionals would have been unlikely to be able to generate. There were also two cases where public sector scientists who were recipients of academic outreach ended up using their context-specific expertise to contribute to the analysis and advancement of the academic research. In both of these cases, my research was able to trace how outreach leads to other forms of boundary transaction, such as collaborative research and boundary-spanning, as in both cases the non-academic scientist ended up co-authoring research papers and eventually given academic positions.

Some instances of outreach directly aim to connect with members of the public and these could advance academia's research or teaching mission at the same time as their third mission. In addition to the conservation management project, mentioned earlier, there is an example of an astronomy research programme whose outreach activity directly supported the physics department's mission of enhancing its students' employability. Such is the demand for quality science communication amongst informed publics and in schools that outreach activities in these areas can lead to significant opportunities for both staff and students to further their careers. I found several cases of academics and students furthering their careers and gaining nationwide recognition for their outreach, in one case directly leading to the employment of one of the doctoral graduates who had supported the research and led some of its related outreach activities.

The main function of outreach is to initiate new networks which, in the longer term, may develop into more intensive forms of relations and transactions. But it can also have immediate benefits, not only to the recipients of outreach, but, in a significant minority of instances, to the advancement of academic missions. Indeed, it could be argued that outreach is the single most valuable form of boundary transaction because it manages to achieve much whilst remaining relatively 'light touch' and 'low cost', rarely throwing up significant boundary management issues or challenges to academia's identity or values (unless and until it develops into more intensive forms of transaction).

2. Collaborative research

In the first section of this chapter, all three case studies showed a tendency for the research and related activities to become more application oriented as the programme of research developed. This was a general finding across my whole sample. It might therefore be expected that relationships between academics and non-academics that develop to the point where they jointly produce knowledge – indicated by the co-authorship of research outputs – would emerge towards the latter stages of the research. This is because, by this stage, the research would be more likely to be ready for dissemination to users, and likely to be a less uncertain and risky project from the perspective of non-academic collaborators, particularly industry actors thinking about proximity to market. Interestingly, in my sampled programmes of research, collaborative research and authorship are almost just as likely at the early stages as they are at the latter stages. When studying my sampled programmes of research, I broke each down into an 'early', 'middle' and 'latter' stage based on key temporal and epistemic milestones within each programme, not because of any a priori theory about how research progresses, but just in order to account for the possibility that boundary relations may change over time in the context of a dynamic programme of research. Based on these stages, I found that eight of my sampled programmes of research included co-authored papers at the 'early' and 'middle' stages, with only a slight increase to nine at the 'latter' stage (see Table 3.1). Note that they were not the same eight or nine cases at each stage; a total of 11 cases (58%) involved co-authorship with a non-academic at some point.

This suggests that the intensive boundary transaction that is co-production of knowledge and co-authorship of research is not only something that happens at the 'development' stage of research, but also something that happens at far earlier and more 'basic' stages of research. The closest and longest-term collaborations seemed to be with not-for-profit collaborators. For example, in four cases focused on health contexts, medical practitioners were named as co-authors at all three stages of the research, as was also the case in two cases involving collaborations with public science bodies. However, profit-motivated collaborations also sometimes came at the earliest stages of research, as was the case in two programmes of research involving collaborations with scientists based in the pharmaceutical industry. In only three cases did co-authorship occur *solely* at the final stage and, even in these cases, co-authorship was a manifestation of a longer-lasting relationship.

As discussed in Chapter 2, collaboration can be a particularly intensive and costly form of boundary transaction in the sense that it can put academics into contexts where their academic values, goals and identities blur with those of industry, and where their research activity goes beyond what some would consider the proper boundaries of academic research, even

Table 3.1 Frequency of cases with collaboration (co-authorship) by 'stage'

Stage	Early	Middle	Latter	Total
Number of cases	8	8	9	11

contributing to a trend towards a 'postacademic' science. My findings indeed show that very close academic/non-academic collaborations can exist, with non-academic collaborators often becoming involved in the early, 'basic' stages of academic research, and not merely entering into collaboration in the final stages when there is a clear promise of extracting benefit from the research. In Chapter 4, I present an analysis from a more macro-level perspective which highlights such risks to academic boundaries of engaging in such close collaborative relationships. However, from the perspective taken within the present chapter, it is also the case that non-academic involvement can contribute much to (i) the fulfilment of departments' long-term academic and disciplinary research, and (ii) the reinforcement or enhancement of the university's privileged and distinctive position as society's core knowledge institution (Etzkowitz, 2008).

3. User-oriented outputs

User-oriented outputs took three distinct forms, what I refer to as *technological outputs, user-focused publications* and *bridging concepts*. The most common form was *technological outputs*, such as patented technologies or techniques, software or online tools. These were mostly associated with departments which were either clearly basic or clearly applied in their research orientation, rather than departments which were use-inspired basic. In later chapters I discuss the reasons for use-inspired basic research being relatively less reliant on technological outputs, but for now I just note an interesting difference between the basic and applied departments' uses of technological outputs. Technological outputs from the basic science departments (including biology, physics and mathematics) tended to take the form of software or online tools designed to support analysis and visualisation of complex, spatiotemporal data. In each case they not only aided 'users' of the outputs but were also central to the academics' own research. By contrast, technological outputs from the applied departments (including metallurgy and materials and computer science) normally resulted in patented technological devices and techniques, and normally did not feed back into the research process but were solely the outputs of research. Again, I further discuss this difference in future chapters.

The second most common user-oriented output was *user-focused publications*. Again, a very similar kind of variation emerges between the outputs of basic and applied departments, albeit with fewer cases. In two cases from basic science departments (such as Case 2 in the first section of this chapter), academic outputs (such as journal articles and books) were published which provided descriptions of methodological and technological innovations and their wider potential applications. The intention was not only to inform practice, but also to inform further research in neighbouring disciplines or sub-disciplinary specialisms. By contrast, in the more applied disciplines, user-focused publications were more likely to take the form of briefings or guidelines for direct application in policy or practice, and therefore, like the technological outputs from applied disciplines, had less possibility of informing further research.

The final form is what I call *bridging concepts*. These are concepts which condense scientific research and theory into a more readily understandable concept so as to be suitable for consideration and application by users and stakeholders. They are most prevalent and significant in research from the use-inspired basic sciences, for reasons I discuss in future chapters. One instance is the concept of 'assimilative capacity', used in ecological research to refer to the level of change that a given natural environment could assimilate before being considered a negative change requiring action. Another is the concept of 'serotonin syndrome', which was used in the field of psychopharmacology (discussed in Case 3) and refers to a continuum of negative effects associated with given levels of build-up of serotonin caused by drug intake. Both these concepts have 'bridged' underpinning science to inform the development and application of policy and advice.

I have here highlighted some variation by epistemic content. This line of discussion is addressed again later, particularly in Chapter 5. To summarise this form of boundary transaction, it is instructive to consider again the timing of user-oriented outputs. What we see is, as with 'collaboration', user-oriented outputs did not, as might have been expected, occur only at the later stages of research – they are not just culminations of research; still less are they merely add-ons to the research. Rather, user-oriented outputs are often important throughout the whole research process, particularly in the case of basic research where user-oriented outputs are not solely user-oriented but also function to advance the research itself. Almost exactly mirroring 'collaboration', there are six programmes of research which produce user-oriented outputs at the 'early' and 'middle' stages of research and only a slight increase to seven at the 'latter' stage (see Table 3.2).

Again, in isolation it is not possible to make inferences about what this pattern of user-oriented outputs means for the long-term reproduction or weakening of academic boundaries. However, it does show that consideration of use(rs) is an important driver of much of the research sampled and

Table 3.2 Frequency of cases of user-oriented outputs by 'stage'

Stage	Early	Middle	Latter	Total
Number of cases	6	6	7	11

is often intertwined with the epistemic content and objectives of research from an early stage. Again, boundary transactions can simultaneously give something to wider society whilst also being incorporated into a distinctive academic research mission and thereby act as a mechanism for simultaneously crossing and reinforcing academic boundaries.

4. Boundary structures

The boundary structures identified in my study can be further broken down into three more specific forms that I refer to as *formal partnerships*, *transdisciplinary structures* and *economic structures*. Formal partnerships refer to structures that formally join the activities of an academic and non-academic organisation. This is distinct from merely a collaboration between members of two different organisations. My own sampled research included two relatively common forms of formal partnership – the medical school and the university-industry consortium – and both proved capable of contributing to the reinforcement of academic boundaries in the sense that they allowed new opportunities for academia to advance its core missions and enact academic values and identities, albeit that such partnerships are not free of transaction costs. In the case of medical schools, my research found that they are increasingly sites not only of the teaching and training of doctors, but of the simultaneous advancement of all three missions of teaching, research and their 'third mission' of real-world impact. There may be a 'cost' of ceding some control over the way in which these missions are fulfilled, but they nonetheless provide universities with enhanced and enriched opportunities for fulfilling them. In the case of university-industry consortia, industry members pay a fee to enter the consortium in return for benefits such as being able to shape and learn from academic research. Again, although 'costly' in that this inevitably means ceding control over the direction and conduct of academic research, they also help to advance academia's core research by providing the academic department with access to long-term insider problems, new data that would otherwise be unavailable and injections of cash that can be used to help sustain long-term research programmes. More subtly, they provide a way for academics to emphasise and enact their distinctive positions and identities by acting as the disinterested, non-profit-seeking anchor which brings together businesses within a forum where they can temporarily suspend their competition and where data and ideas can be shared for the mutual benefit of the member businesses and, at least in the two cases in my sample, to the wider public, since both consortia primarily centred around making industry 'greener' and/or cleaner for the environment and for the industry's customers.

Transdisciplinary structures are the most frequent form of boundary structure and refer to structures designed to link researchers to actors and organisations closer to contexts of use. The term 'transdisciplinary structure' emphasises that, although committed to advancing research, they transcend allegiance to a specific traditional discipline and rather draw on any relevant expertise in pursuit of wider societal or economic objectives (Gibbons et al., 1994; Nowotny, 2006). In some cases, transdisciplinary structures become key coordinating structures housing academics in ways which rival their allegiance to disciplinary departments. In other cases, they are add-on structures which academics are linked to in addition to core research units, such as relatively formal 'networks' or 'centres' which may have some presence, such as a website, but do not institutionalise the commitment of specific external organisations in the same way that 'formal partnerships' (discussed earlier) do. All three case studies discussed in the first half of this chapter happened to be based on research conducted within transdisciplinary structures. Therefore, I will not provide further discussion and examples here.

Lastly, *economic structures* include structures such as technology transfer offices, university-owned management companies and academic spin-outs, whose objectives are to directly intervene in the market and generate revenue and sometimes even personal profit, as was the case in Case 1. However, the second case study included an example of how even economic structures can contribute to core academic missions, as a spin-out company was created to sell academic technologies, with all profits being fed back into the unit's core research. In another example from my research, not only were all the profits from the research unit's spin-out consultancy company fed back into their core research, but the consultancy work itself sometimes led to new and intellectually challenging lines of academic research and publications, therefore showing how boundary transactions can contribute epistemically as well as financially to academia's core missions.

To summarise, boundary structures can be understood as universities' attempts to regulate their boundaries and their place in society. They provide universities with ways of simultaneously serving external and internal purposes, thereby reinforcing and re-legitimating the university's distinct position. As Figure 3.2 shows, almost all the boundary structures identified made clear contributions to at least one of academia's core missions of research, the teaching/training of students, or both, with only two of the identified boundary structures not exhibiting a clear contribution to either core mission.

5. *Boundary-spanners*

Boundary-spanners appear in 13 of the sampled programmes of research. Boundary-spanners in my sample include people with a range of different

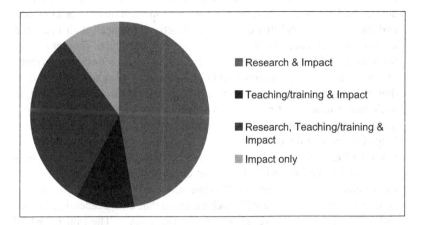

Figure 3.2 Pie chart showing boundary structures contributing to different missions

trajectories. For example, boundary-spanners might be students/recent graduates, senior academics who had a short period in non-academic roles, or scientists from outside academia but who go on to take up academic posts. I will discuss these different kinds of boundary-spanners.

One example of students/graduates as boundary-spanners was in the interdisciplinary field of marine conservation ecology, with much research being conducted in tropical coastal regions and communities. Several of the centre's research students are international and already have professional conservation roles in their home countries. Their research simultaneously extends and applies the centre's core research. Such was their importance that students/graduates co-authored two-thirds of the papers which I encountered in my study of this programme of research. In another case, a research centre in an applied sub-field of chemistry had developed such close links and alignment with a specific unit of a large pharmaceutical company that, as of 2014, 15 of the centre's doctoral graduates had taken up roles there, making up half of the unit's workforce. In two different cases of mathematics research, a large part of the impact depended on PhD graduates bringing new statistical or analytical techniques developed with their academic supervisors into applied, non-academic contexts (one related to data linkage in the NHS, the other related to spatial analysis in the oil and gas industry).

Instances of what I call *outwardly mobile* academic boundary-spanners, that is, career academics who have either additional or short-term roles outside academia, took two main forms in my sample. Essentially these two forms are industrial and non-industrial. In the industrial cases, academics had previously held short-term roles in an industrial or commercial environment, and this experience directly influenced their approach to academic research in ways that made the particular programme of research possible. For example, in two cases, the short industry experience of academics gave academics insight into the needs of industry which they then used to their advantage when focusing their research (engineering, in both cases) in areas of relevance which attracted support from both academic and industrial sponsors. In another case, the industrial experience helped the academic to understand the needs of the sector, and this unique combination of industry knowledge and academic position gave the academic the credibility and insight to set up an academic-industry consortia where competing businesses within the sector collaborated with both the academic department and with each other, so that both academic research and industry impact were advanced simultaneously. The non-industrial form of *outwardly mobile* boundary-spanning occurred in two cases in my sample. These cases bore resemblance to outreach, but went well beyond this, as academics took up roles not only to advise, but to actively promote policies related to the environment, for example, via roles with NGOs and charities.

Lastly, I identified three instances of what I call *inward mobility*, where a non-academic scientist came to take up a role within the university that was associated with advancing the department's impact. In two cases, the inward mobility took the form of non-academic collaborators being given either honorary or part-time appointments to recognise or consolidate the important research contribution that this non-academic had made. The third case is interesting in that it closely resembles but is subtly different from the case mentioned earlier of the *outwardly mobile* boundary-spanner who then set up an academic-industry consortium. The difference in this case is that the department, presumably lacking an academic internally with sufficiently close links to industry, 'bought in' these links by appointing a scientist with three decades' industry experience to a professorship in order to direct the consortium, rather than the consortium being set up by a current academic.

As the last case shows, there are often significant transaction costs associated with boundary-spanning, particularly where it means ceding control over the direction of research or the training and teaching of students to industry actors. However, overall, Figure 3.3 shows that the vast majority of cases of boundary-spanning in my sample simultaneously contributed to either the research mission, teaching mission or both, as well as to non-academic impact.

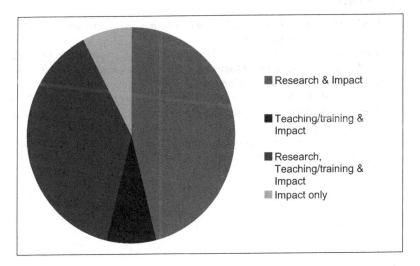

Figure 3.3 Pie chart showing boundary-spanning contributing to different missions

Summary

This chapter focused the boundary lens to zoom in on empirical data from two different perspectives. The first section presented an analysis of three in-depth, illustrative case studies (selected from my larger sample) to show the functioning and effects of boundary transactions in 'unbounded', 'moderately bounded' and 'bounded' programmes of academic STEMM research, taken from the fields of computer science, marine biology and psychobiology, respectively. The second part of the chapter shifted focus to zoom in on the five main forms of boundary transactions. Here, I analysed each form of boundary transaction across the sample as a whole and elaborated on how they served the kinds of functions seen in the three illustrative case studies. The findings of the combined analyses suggest that the boundary transactions in my sampled research are, for the most part, enactments of rather than digressions from academic identities and values, and that they are operating as intended from the university's perspective – that is, to *regulate* academia's relations to society, leading to the reproduction of boundaries that are neither excessively strong and closed-off, nor excessively open and weak. However, caution is needed regarding this apparently positive finding, for reasons further discussed in Chapters 4 and 5.

References

Etzkowitz, H. (2008). *The triple helix: University-industry-government innovation in action.* New York: Routledge.

Gibbons, M., Limoges, C., Nowotny, H., Schwartzman, S., Scott, P., & Trow, M. (1994). *The new production of knowledge: The dynamics of science and research in contemporary societies.* London: Sage.

McNie, E. C., Parris, A., & Sarewitz, D. (2016). Improving the public value of science: A typology to inform discussion, design and implementation of research. *Research Policy, 45*(4), 884–895. doi:10.1016/j.respol.2016.01.004

Nowotny, H. (2006). *The potential of transdisciplinarity.* Retrieved from www.helga-nowotny.eu/downloads/helga_nowotny_b59.pdf

4 Zoom out
The knowledge society through the boundary lens

Academia is part of a knowledge society, or what some have started to refer to as a knowledge 'ecology' (Barnett, 2017; Wright, 2016), emphasising the interrelatedness and interdependence of its different sectors and actors. This concept helps to emphasise that academia simply cannot exist in a way which removes itself from these interrelations and interdependencies, even if it wanted to. As I will show in this chapter, there are a range of forces that academia, by its existence, is bound to participate in and be influenced by. These forces bring academia into necessary and unavoidable boundary relations with the world in various ways. But this does not mean that they are entirely beyond academia's control. I showed in Chapter 3 how academic institutions and actors could exert more or less control over specific instances of boundary transaction. Similarly, an analysis of these forces through the boundary lens construes them as 'boundary forces', that is, forces which confront and interact with academic boundaries and which can be sustained or changed through the mechanism of boundary transactions. This chapter will show that academia can exert more or less control over these boundary forces, so that it is not predetermined whether they will lead to the eventual undermining of academic boundaries or rather to their ongoing legitimacy.

I organise the discussion of these 'ecology-level' boundary forces under three broad themes: 'educational function', 'academic identity' and 'knowledge regimes'.

The educational function

(Doctoral) graduates in non-academic, knowledge-intensive sectors

Several scholars have analysed the relationship between academia's research and teaching functions, often finding them moving in opposing directions, as universities institute a division of labour whereby some academics focus on research and other academics conduct most of the teaching. But there remain complex ways in which the research and teaching functions of universities interact with and influence one another. In particular, the educational function of universities plays various roles in shaping how academia relates to the knowledge ecology through its research activities and research-related boundary transactions.

One of the most important ways this takes place is through the mobility of graduates, especially doctoral graduates, into knowledge-intensive sectors. The majority of STEMM doctoral graduates leave academia – either immediately or after some postdoctoral period – to work in some other knowledge-intensive sector (Royal Society, 2010). These highly academically trained graduates bring their academic skills, knowledge and mindsets into non-academic knowledge-intensive sectors, from within which these individuals have the capacity and incentive to demand, absorb, apply and occasionally even collaborate on new academic science. As others have noted (e.g., Etzkowitz, 2008; Gibbons et al., 1994), universities' proficiency in providing higher education, particularly in producing doctoral graduates for non-academic sectors, has therefore played a significant role in contributing to the pressures faced by academia to engage in greater boundary transactions and steer their activities towards non-academic objectives. This is reflected in the research-related boundary transactions I investigated for this book, most of which involved academics interacting with STEMM doctoral graduates based in non-academic, knowledge-intensive organisations. But as well as contributing to boundary pressures by contributing to the external demands made on academia, this outflow of graduates into non-academic sectors can also serve as a mechanism through which academia can exert control over its boundary transactions and ensure that its boundary transactions function to reinforce rather than undermine academic boundaries. One of the things that became clear when researching for this book was that, by focusing their boundary transaction efforts towards organisations and sectors that were replete with academic expertise in the form of doctoral graduates, academics were able to reduce the 'costs' associated with transactions (see the discussion of transaction costs in Chapters 2 and 5). This occurred through two main mechanisms.

The first mechanism I identified is the easing of interpersonal communication. The existence of these highly academically trained graduates in non-academic organisations meant that the people involved, despite being in very different kinds of organisations, had something in common as both had experienced significant academic 'socialisation' into 'esoteric' knowledge domains (Bernstein, 2000, pp. 11, 29). This immediately reduces the costs of transaction because it reduces the time needed to establish a shared understanding and rapport. In effect, this creates a situation whereby boundary-crossing transactions may not be experienced so much like boundary-crossing at all, but more like a collaboration with an academic colleague. Something of the 'academic' has entered and merged with the 'non-academic', in a sense extending the reach of academic boundaries. While the result is a blurring of boundaries between academic and non-academic sectors, it is not necessarily a blurring which impinges on existing academic boundaries and values, but rather one which, at least under certain conditions, creates a new space, a kind of 'free trade zone', where 'low-cost' boundary transactions can take place between similarly minded individuals, both of whom can simultaneously contribute to one another's institutional missions without significantly threatening the distinctive identity or core boundaries of either. As I discussed in relation to boundary-spanners in Chapter 3, the positive effects of this can be especially significant in cases where doctoral graduates are directly applying work related to the expertise of their doctoral research unit and where they continue to collaborate with their previous academic department from the context of their new, non-academic context.

A second mechanism by which transaction costs are reduced is through the increased 'absorptive capacity', that is, the ability of non-academic organisations and systems (or more specifically, the individuals within them) 'to identify, assimilate and apply' external knowledge (Bishop, D'Este, & Neely, 2011, p. 31; see also Ternouth, Herrmann, & Docherty, 2010). While this has obvious benefits for the knowledge objectives of the organisations, it can also benefit academia. Where academia is engaged in boundary transactions with an organisation or sector with a lower absorptive capacity, they may need to take the time and effort to find new ways of codifying and transmitting knowledge that can be understood and applied more easily. By contrast, engaging with organisations or sectors with a higher absorptive capacity allows academia to achieve boundary transactions without making significant changes to its mode of knowledge production and transmission. Many of the user-oriented outputs discussed in Chapter 3 would not have been possible were it not for sufficient absorptive capacity in relevant non-academic sectors.

Teaching and training for employability

So far, this section has focused on the effects and implications of doctoral graduates as they enter non-academic, knowledge-intensive professions. However, the educational function of universities can influence academia's boundary relations in a more immediate (and arguably more fundamental) sense. The need for academics to think about the employability of their students puts some boundary pressures on academia because it requires them to find ways of incorporating the needs and demands of external organisations (i.e., potential employers of their students) when planning their students' training and learning opportunities. My research found that academics' responsibility to promote the employability of their doctoral students often prompted them to seek out boundary transactions that students could be involved in for the advancement of their education and employability. Again, such a situation could in principle serve to undermine academia's distinctive identity if its educational provision comes to be overly determined by non-academic interests, with potentially weakening effects on academia's boundedness. However, it is possible for academia to take control over student-/graduate-based boundary transactions by using them as opportunities to reinforce its own distinctive identity, missions and value(s). This could be achieved by orienting students' research or project work towards areas that are relevant to potential employers but at the same time contribute substantively to the department's core research agenda. This is precisely what happened in several of the cases mentioned in Chapter 3, where I identified 'boundary-spanning' research students who conducted projects within industry or public sector organisations and, as a result of the knowledge and skills acquired, became employed in that organisation after graduation. Interestingly, four of the academics I interviewed for this book, each of whom had once worked as a non-academic researcher, explained that doctoral students' eagerness to work hard and learn new skills was one of the major factors persuading them to return to academia because these traits made doctoral student supervisees an excellent resource to boost the academic's own research capacity.

Overall, the educational function of academia, particularly at the doctoral level, does not simply sit alongside the research function, but interacts with the research function in both direct and indirect ways. The need for students' future employability to be considered, and the knowledge demands that highly trained graduates make on academia once they are employed in knowledge-intensive sectors, contribute to the boundary pressures facing academia and potentially undermining academic boundaries. But it is possible for academia to exert control over these relations such that they instead serve to reinforce these boundaries. The various departments and programmes of research I have studied for this book appear to have achieved this with some success.

Academic identity

Institutional level

Although the notion of 'academic identity' seems initially to steer the analysis inwards rather than outwards to the knowledge society or 'ecology', I argue that the notion of academic identity is not purely internal but rather is partly constituted by external social actors and their relations with academia. There are both institutional and individual levels to the concept of academic identity. I will start by discussing the former.

In his lectures on the emergence and development of the European university, Émile Durkheim (2013) spoke of the university's '*sui generis*' (p. 93, original emphasis) driving force or trajectory, which he described as

> a profound feeling . . . that the university would never fulfil its true destiny, would never achieve its true identity except in so far as it comprised a plurality or even the totality of the branches of human learning. It was . . . an ideal . . . towards which the university strove and was expected to strive. This is what we must not overlook if we wish to understand accurately the formation and development of the university. Over and above the external factors which brought it into existence and however these contingent factors affected it, as they certainly did with respect to the organisation of the university, there was still an *internal* phenomenon without which they would have remained more or less sterile.

Here, Durkheim is arguing that the most significant explanatory factor underpinning the university's development is its own internal drive to *objectify* the world, that is, to internalise the outside world (natural and social) into objects of academic knowledge. The predominant form that this internalisation of the external has taken is the proliferation of ever more finely specified academic disciplines, including inter- and sub-disciplinary fields.

However, and crucially for my argument that academic identity is constituted not only within academia but also through academia's boundary relations, this proliferation and expansion of academic disciplines has always developed in ways partly determined by external needs and academia's willingness to be influenced by them. The contemporary impact agenda (along with similar agendas for academic research, and science more generally) highlights that the direction of academic research is increasingly determined by what is perceived to be of relevance to key 'external publics' (Putnam, 2009, p. 127) who provide societal and financial support for new research. But this is by no means an entirely new phenomenon, as a consideration of the history of the research function of universities shows. For example, the emergence of empirical science (then referred to as 'natural philosophy') as a central component of the European university in the period of the fifteenth to the seventeenth century coincided precisely with the emergence of societal demands for just such knowledge, first amongst the artists, architects and engineers of Italy and then, even more extensively, amongst the new middle class of navigators, merchants and artisans of Northern Europe (Ben-David, 1971). Similarly, when the more significant expansion of the academic research profession began in early-nineteenth-century Germany, this was prompted, in large part, by external expansions in knowledge-intensive industry, as well as by the efforts of academic scientists to create closer linkages with these industries, both through the content of their research and through the content of the (research-based) training received by their students (Ben-David, 1971, 1977).

In light of this history, Bresnen and Burrell (2013) have proposed the notion of a 'Mode 0' system of knowledge production that precedes and to some extent subsumes Modes 1 and 2 (Gibbons et al., 1994). The 'Mode 0' thesis emphasises that science has always exhibited a responsiveness to external knowledge demands and that academic disciplines have often developed through forms of patronage whereby the insulated space for conducting empirical research and constructing bounded disciplinary categories and identities co-evolved with, and relied on, the willingness of socially powerful actors to sponsor such work. This chimes with some of the empirical findings of my own research and others that where there is promise of a long-term, mutually beneficial relationship, university-industry collaboration can be compatible with and even contribute to 'academic freedom' (Slaughter, Archerd, & Campbell, 2004, p. 146) to the extent that it provides the resources and forms of capital which are important to the conduct of good-quality science that might otherwise have not been possible.

Framing this all through the boundary lens – zoomed out to focus on ecological level transactions – we can characterise the situation as follows. Academia '*transcodes* external issues and influences into topics of its own' (Kantasalmi & Tuunainen, 2018, p. 354, original emphasis) in order to enact and advance its own sui generis identity and purpose of construing the external world as internally legitimate objects of academic (and more specifically, disciplinary) knowledge. This 'exchange relationship' (Kogan, 2000, p. 215), in which academia, on the one hand, *receives* from non-academic sectors new objects of knowledge (as well as social and financial support for the study of such objects) and, on the other, *gives* new knowledge relevant to these non-academic sectors, is an example of what organisational sociology construes as the 'performances each system delivers for other systems' (Kantasalmi & Tuunainen, 2018, p. 354), especially in the context of a knowledge ecology. At the institutional level then, academic identity, however bounded and inward-looking it may appear on the surface, is necessarily intertwined and partly constituted by its relation to the external.

Individual level

Earlier, I argued that the institutional-level notion of academic identity inevitably brings about boundary pressures on academia because, throughout history, academia has enacted and realised its distinctive institutional identity in part by internalising and addressing the needs and interests of external publics. At the individual level, the boundary pressures arise from the broad and contested meaning of what the marker of 'academic' denotes about a person's identity, that is, the varying norms and values associated with what it means to be an academic and the expectations and perceptions that academics have of themselves and, just as important but less often discussed, that others have of them.

The first claim made in the preceding paragraph, that the notion of 'academic identity' is broad and contested, able to accommodate many different interpretations, is best evidenced by a comparison of two of my interview respondents. The two interviewees were both professors whose research could be broadly classified as user-oriented life science. More specifically, both worked in areas directly related to marine ecosystems and both engaged in a broad range of boundary transactions which involved policymakers, non-governmental organisations, the private sector and, occasionally, the general public. Their research often touched on highly contested issues where economic and environmental concerns frequently clashed. But despite these significant similarities, these academics' respective senses of identity were profoundly different and led to vastly different approaches to boundary transactions. One of the professors defined their academic identity solely in terms of objectivity and scientific rigour, and made a point about *not* going beyond scientific advice and into the realm of policy advocacy or any form of activism:

> You find yourself in the middle of very enthusiastic political debate, with vehement beliefs on one side and the other. And then there's people like me who try to put that to one side when doing the science. So you're under fire from both sides. . . . You're ploughing the middle way through the interest groups which are quite polarized. . . . And we provide the information. And not everyone agrees with this, but for me I'm absolutely clear that we provide the science, we don't advise on policy.
> (Interviewee)

In complete contrast, the other professor spoke passionately about how their academic and scientific identities were, to an extent, subsumed or subservient to their identity as an activist:

> I am speaking effectively as an 'activist' rather than a 'scientist'. And I think that's a blurred distinction for a lot of us. . . . You have to suggest action which means you step across that line between disinterested science and advocacy.
> (Interviewee)

But it is not only academics who have a sense of academic identity. Wider society also holds ideas about the identities of academics, such as the norms and values which they carry and represent, and these can influence expectations about academics and how individual academics are perceived in the context of boundary transactions (Henkel, 2004). Perceptions about the values and the credibility embodied in the identities of individual academics can also be an important part of the reason why non-academic actors seek out academics. Previous research has shown that the credibility associated with academics can sometimes be as or even more important than specific research findings in aligning academics with user groups or other kinds of stakeholders (Bansal, Bertels, Ewart, MacConnachie, & O'Brien, 2012; Meagher, Lyall, & Nutley, 2008). The externally held perception of academics' 'scientific credibility' can serve as a form of 'social capital' (McNie, 2007, pp. 20, 24; see also Ponomariov & Boardman, 2010, p. 617), making academics accepted and desirable contributors to addressing important social, political and economic problems and debates.

Of course, external perceptions of academics are not all completely positive and do not always lend themselves to being immediately trustful of academics. Where this is the case, more deliberate and potentially costly efforts are required to translate scientific capital into credibility/trust – what Cordner (2015, p. 916) calls 'strategic science translation'. For example, one of my interviewees spoke of their experience of outreach activity which led them to enter spaces used by people with mental health problems, explaining that some people in those spaces do not always welcome academics because they can be perceived as just being 'about the publication' rather than 'with a genuine interest to understand and help'. The interviewee therefore emphasised that 'you need to gain trust of everyone you work with and accept that you have to do something for them, that clearly benefits them, even though sometimes they're not ready or willing to see that'. Another of my interview respondents made similar points, explaining that some people, particularly where research and boundary transactions bring academics into relation with local communities and members of the general public, will only begin to trust academics once they recognise that the academic is willing to make a long-term commitment. 'For us, trust is essential. And that only comes through long-term commitment and exposure'. The same interviewee went onto illustrate that even after several years when a decent level of trust had been established, there could still be barriers to achieving a fully mutual understanding and alignment:

> Now, in my head, [I was doing] 'applied science' because the model that lots of scientists use is we look at . . . problems and then we publish a paper that says '[X] are important because they support [Y] and

[Y] are important because they support people, end of story', and then we've done our bit. However, that's a very naïve theory of change. ... From the perspective of the local people I wasn't bringing benefits to them. I thought I was ... but after three or four years they said, 'What are you doing for us?' And that was a shock, because it was a very pleasant place to work and they were friendly. But they wanted more from me than that.

(Interviewee)

Thus, external understandings and perceptions of academics' identity and motivations could pose challenges. Another potential challenge is where the credibility associated with the academic identity is mobilised by external actors for their own purposes. For example, non-academics in some professions may want to engage with academics primarily because it provides a boost to their own professional credibility (Hoffman, 2011) rather than because of genuine benefits that arise from the interaction. Of course, even where the non-academic's motivation is to boost their own career and professional credibility, genuine benefits may also occur – one of my interview respondents spoke of their attempts to get a new medical device trialled in a hospital where one of the consultants in particular was initially sceptical and uninterested but, after hearing from nurses about the rapid and significant benefits of the device, the consultant 'became our biggest convert' and now 'believes he'll make his name from [it]', in the words of my interviewee. But sometimes, interactions with academics appear to be somewhat disingenuous attempts to mobilise academic credibility. For example, another of my interview respondents referred to themselves as being 'quite the "token" scientist' when recalling their invitation to participate in a forum to discuss politically contested issues to which their scientific expertise was relevant, suggesting that they saw the academic's presence as adding credibility to the debate without necessarily taking the scientific advice seriously.

Moore (2013) and Beck (2010) build on Bernstein's insight that academic identity has two faces pointing in opposing directions, like a coin (Bernstein, 2000) or the Roman god Janus, 'the god of doorways and hinges, of turning points and openings, of transitions' (Moore, 2013, p. 114). Academic identity embodies the link between the inwardness or boundedness of the university – where academic objectivity and credibility is located – and its outwardness or unboundedness – where academia interacts with wider society both to assert and enact its authority and power as a key knowledge institution and to provide services and benefits to society through the application or exchange of academic knowledge and expertise. This duality of the academic identity gives it a flexibility of meaning that varies depending on different people's perspectives, interests and motivations. For example, when academic input is sought after, the external actor can appeal to the outward-facing character of academic identity in order to partake of and benefit from the credibility and expertise associated with its inward-facing character; that is, they seek out academics to lend their expertise, or at least the symbolic credibility associated with their expertise. Conversely, when an external actor resists or distrusts academic input, the same inward-facing character that others associate with credibility is instead associated with academia's disinterestedness and aloofness, and the need to overcome this distrust raises the costs of academics' boundary transactions.

The duality and flexibility inherent in the notion of individual-level academic identity therefore has the potential to put pressure on academic boundaries. Where the academic identity is exploited simply for its symbolic credibility rather than for the genuine value of academic expertise, the basis for academia's legitimacy is undermined. And when academic identity is perceived not as symbolic of credibility but rather as aloofness from disinterestedness in the 'real world', this also casts doubt on academia's legitimacy and pressures academics to move outside their comfort zone and find new, potentially more costly and non-traditional ways to engage with and gain the trust of external publics. For example, the interviewee I quoted earlier who felt shocked to find that the community he had been working with for several years did not feel that the research had benefited them sufficiently took this as an opportunity to think more creatively and drastically about how he could achieve genuine benefits, prompting him to found a new, more intensively collaborative community project and a new charity dedicated not only to advancing the research objectives but also to generating revenue directly for the community.

However, despite the challenges associated with the expectations, demands and uses made of individual-level academic identity by external actors, my research finds that the credibility and value(s) associated with academic identity function primarily to ease academic boundary transactions. More often than not, the academics involved in the sampled programmes of research and related boundary transactions were received as well-meaning, credible experts with much to contribute, even in cases where there might be disagreement between the academics' views and those of other stakeholders. And where challenges are faced, the flexibility of the meaning of academic identity takes on a further benefit. Academic identity is a suitably powerful and loosely defined (self-)concept that heterogeneous academics can use their own idiosyncratic sense of their academic identity as a motivation to overcome internal and external challenges to achieve diverse research goals and boundary-transacting objectives, so that boundary transactions, and the challenges associated with them, are a way to enact and realise their academic identities. My inferences about individual-level academic identity are, though, very tentative at this stage. My research initially adopted a somewhat more structuralist view of identity (e.g., Bernstein, 2000, pp. 52–79), and this was appropriate since I did not originally set out to study individual perceptions and experiences of academic identity. However, the concept, particularly at the individual level, became important to the book to the extent that it emerged as central to understanding some of my data. Therefore, a more systematic study of individual-level academic identity, following in the footsteps of research that centralises the perceptions, experiences and narratives of individuals (e.g., Archer, 2008; Chubb & Watermeyer, 2017; Watermeyer, 2015, 2016), is still required in order to fully incorporate it into the boundary lens.

Knowledge regimes

As discussed throughout this book, particularly in the literature review section of Chapter 2, academia intersects with and shares interdependencies with other knowledge sectors and systems. However, to the extent that these systems are governed by and geared towards the 'powered, structured interests' (Papatsiba & Cohen, 2020, p. 220) of the actors involved, they can be thought of as relatively distinct 'knowledge regimes' (Bleiklie & Byrkjeflot, 2002, p. 530) that, although also sharing interdependencies, have their own distinctive rules, missions and values. And to the extent that these intersect with universities, there is likely to be a boundary pressure on academia to realign with these other knowledge regimes.

My research is able to dissect and disaggregate the channels through which academia interacts with two of these systems or 'regimes' – the Mode 2 knowledge production system and the 'technoscientific' system. Specifically, I shall argue that the objectives of applied academic science tends to lead to linkages and interdependencies with the Mode 2 system, while those of basic science tends to lead to linkages and interdependencies with the technoscientific system.

Mode 2 knowledge production system

Several of the programmes of research that I analysed for this book, at least at certain points in their progress, exhibited characteristics of and linkages with a Mode 2 system of knowledge production. As discussed earlier, Mode 2 refers to a mode of science where some of academia's traditional values, criteria, organisational forms and even epistemic objectives are left behind in favour of a different set of values, forms and objectives (Gibbons et al., 1994; Nowotny, Scott, & Gibbons, 2003; Ziman, 1996a). At these moments, academics' engagement with the world no longer occurs through or for the advancement of their academic discipline but rather through the contribution of their expertise to localised or specific real-world problems which bring together a transdisciplinary (and often transient) range of actors with various interests and various forms of scientific and non-scientific expertise. This was most commonly apparent in the applied science departments studied. Interviewees from these departments expressed sentiments such as, 'It's an applied subject. To be of any good, somebody has to use it'. Some of these applied scientists had internalised this Mode 2, almost 'postacademic' (Ziman, 1996a) mindset more than others and expressed little interest in reaching out to disciplinary networks at all. For example, one explained, 'There's tonnes of others who might be interested in the work we do but . . . the people I want to influence are clinicians. . . . If the work isn't clinically relevant it's kind of pointless'. Another applied scientist no longer even categorised much of their work as 'research': 'So we've tried to move away from a key "research question" and we're offering more of a delivery of findings, so it's not research-oriented as much'. According to these responses, applied scientists in my sample were strongly committed to real-world impacts and adopted a 'what works' approach to achieving them, prioritising outcomes over scientific findings. To them, this did not just mean the successful conduct of 'applied' research which was judged scientifically rigorous by peers; rather, it meant tangible benefits to clinicians and patients, industry, customers and so on. They often had very specific intended outcomes in mind. For example, one of the applied programmes of research centred around understanding the causes of water discolouration; its ultimate aim was not just to advance understanding but to work with industry engineers and management to help them to develop the best-value monitoring and response procedures, with the specific intended outcomes of improving the experiences of water users and reducing the burden of dealing with customer complaints for water companies. In another example, the programme of research centred around improving technologies in robotic/automated locomotion; again, rather than just advancing the technology, the researchers went to great lengths to collaborate with people who would be able to directly use these technologies, which in this case was users of automated wheelchairs, as well as related health and care professionals, all of whom contributed specific expertise to achieve improvements on wheelchair users' experience. In a third example, research focused on how hydrometallurgical principles could be used to harness oxygen flows to aid wound healing; again, not content with just showing proof of concept, this applied scientist was motivated from the beginning by the challenge of building a practical, cost-effective device for healing specific kinds of chronic wounds and ulcers.

It is now more than two decades since the prevalence of a Mode 2 knowledge production system started provoking concerns of postacademic science (Ziman, 1996a) in which universities' research capacity is restricted to contributing to externally generated problems, often short-term and localised, rather than to the advancement of academic disciplines, and to producing knowledge whose 'validity is no longer determined solely, or predominantly, by narrowly circumscribed scientific communities, but by much wider communities of engagement comprising knowledge producers, disseminators, traders, and users' (Nowotny et al., 2003, pp. 191–192). Whatever one's view on the prescience or prematurity of the description of the contemporary science system as postacademic, the broadly distributed network of knowledge actors as described by Nowotny et al. (2003) constitutes a significant force which exists independently of and acts powerfully on – despite (or rather because of) its dependency on and connectedness to – academia. This puts significant boundary pressures on academia in the sense that academia increasingly engages in research and research-related boundary transactions over which it has less control. At these moments, academic disciplines may remain as important founts of knowledge and methodologies, and may be a source of identity, but they are not drivers or organisational anchors of research efforts. Rather, scientific expertise and effort is coordinated around the integrating principle of transdisciplinary and transinstitutional collaboration to find solutions to localised social, economic and technological problems. Academics, particularly those based in applied science departments, are often dependent on acting in at least occasional alignment to and accordance with this Mode 2 knowledge production system, despite its challenge to traditional academic cultures, forms, criteria and values.

Technoscientific system

The notion of a technoscientific system, order or regime refers to the use by powerful political, commercial and military interest groups of their vast resources to mobilise knowledge production systems and institutions to 'control' (Bensaude-Vincent, Loeve, Nordmann, & Schwarz, 2011, p. 366) and 'construct' (Schmidt, 2011, p. 104) the social world (Latour, 1987; Leydesdorff, 2012; Slaughter, Campbell, Holleman, & Morgan, 2002; Ziman, 1996b) according to their own vision and interests. Inevitably, such a mobilisation of resources has its effects on academic research. In my own study, I found that research based in basic science departments often aligned with such technoscientific projects. The reason for this seems to be inherent in the nature of basic scientific research, which is constantly pushing at the frontiers of current knowledge and humanly accessible data and whose discoveries can have far-reaching consequences and implications for a range of different scientific and real-life applications (Ziman, 1984). This desire for new data, allowing ever more fundamental insight into various aspects of the natural world, fuels the demand for technologies capable of accessing and analysing this data, and it is these technologies that then have potentially wider scientific and real-life applicability. This was recognised by the basic scientists I interviewed:

> I think about the science rather than who might end up using it. But the hard work is actually the collection and analysis of the data – our science is driven by the data we can collect. So we have the instrumentation group . . . [whose] instruments allow us to do much more in terms of the science, but then the technology also gets sold all over the world.
>
> (Basic scientist)
>
> Scientists are always going to be playing around with the latest unproven technology . . . but actually there's a synergy rather than a tension between scientific technology and technology for application. Because although it's core science, the components and technology can be used and sold for various other purposes.
>
> (Basic scientist)

This synergy, whereby the demand for technology to drive basic science converges with the social demand for technologies, underpins academia's participation in the technoscientific knowledge system or regime, not least because the technologies driving advances in basic science require access to the kinds of resources underpinning technoscientific power. My study revealed several instances of research based in basic science departments that involved links to and transactions with key technoscientific actors (for a further case study, see also Kantasalmi & Tuunainen, 2018, pp. 348–352). For example, three programmes of basic science research in my sample produced technologies which contributed to national security, including a biology department conducting research supporting naval operations; a chemistry department developing technologies for law enforcement; and a physics department leading European space projects. Similarly, three programmes of research contributed to large energy industry companies, including one chemistry department and one mathematics department that contributed new technologies for the oil and gas exploration and extraction industry, and a physics department contributing technology to international thermonuclear reactor projects.

In these cases, new technologies, just as they push back the frontiers of data collection for scientific purposes, also drive the cutting edge in production for commerce and national security.

Summary

This chapter 'zoomed out' to analyse academia's boundary relations with the knowledge society more widely. No longer focusing on specific boundary transactions, this chapter adopted a more macro-level perspective to analyse the key factors shaping universities' relations with and role within the knowledge society. These included the epistemic content of different branches of science; the orientation towards application or understanding of different programmes of academic research; the demands and power of other key knowledge institutions and sectors that use, collaborate on or sponsor academic research; the fluid meaning of 'academic identity' as constructed by both academics themselves and the users of academic research; and the teaching/training function of academia, which, paradoxically, is probably the most important mechanism for both the reinforcement and re-legitimation of academic boundaries as well as being one of the most important mechanisms through which academic boundaries are pressured and contested.

References

Archer, L. (2008). The new neoliberal subjects? Young/er academics' constructions of professional identity. *Journal of Education Policy, 23*(3), 265–285. doi:10.1080/02680930701754047

Bansal, P., Bertels, S., Ewart, T., MacConnachie, P., & O'Brien, J. (2012). Bridging the research-practice gap. *Academy of Management Perspectives, 26*(1), 73–92. doi:10.5465/amp.2011.0140

Barnett, R. (2017). *The ecological university: A feasible utopia*. London: Routledge.

Beck, J. (2010). Promoting official pedagogic identities: The sacred and the profane. In K. Maton & R. Moore (Eds.), *Social realism, knowledge and the sociology of education: Coalitions of the mind*. London: Continuum.

Ben-David, J. (1971). *The scientist's role in society: A comparative study*. Englewood Cliffs, NJ: Prentice-Hall.

Ben-David, J. (1977). *Centres of learning: Britain, France, Germany, United States*. New York: McGraw Hill.

Bensaude-Vincent, B., Loeve, S., Nordmann, A., & Schwarz, A. (2011). Matters of interest: The objects of research in science and technoscience. *Journal for General Philosophy of Science, 42*(2), 365–383. doi:10.1007/s10838-011-9172-y

Bernstein, B. (2000). *Pedagogy, symbolic control, and identity: Theory, research, critique* (2nd ed.). Oxford: Rowman & Littlefield.

Bishop, K., D'Este, P., & Neely, A. (2011). Gaining from interactions with universities: Multiple methods for nurturing absorptive capacity. *Research Policy, 40*(1), 30–40. doi:10.1016/j.respol.2010.09.009

Bleiklie, I., & Byrkjeflot, H. (2002). Changing knowledge regimes: Universities in a new research environment. *The International Journal of Higher Education and Educational Planning, 44*(3), 519–532. doi:10.1023/A:1019898407492

Bresnen, M., & Burrell, G. (2013). Journals à la mode? Twenty years of living alongside Mode 2 and the new production of knowledge. *Organization, 20*(1), 25–37. doi:10.1177/1350508412460992

Chubb, J., & Watermeyer, R. (2017). Artifice or integrity in the marketization of research impact? Investigating the moral economy of (pathways to) impact statements within research funding proposals in the UK and Australia. *Studies in Higher Education, 42*(12), 2360–2372. doi:10.1080/03075079.2016.1144182

Cordner, A. (2015). Strategic science translation and environmental controversies. *Science, Technology, & Human Values, 40*(6), 915–938. doi:10.1177/0162243915584164

Durkheim, É. (2013). *The evolution of educational thought: Lectures on the formation and development of secondary education in France*. Oxon: Routledge.

Etzkowitz, H. (2008). *The triple helix: University-industry-government innovation in action*. New York: Routledge.

Gibbons, M., Limoges, C., Nowotny, H., Schwartzman, S., Scott, P., & Trow, M. (1994). *The new production of knowledge: The dynamics of science and research in contemporary societies*. London: Sage.

Henkel, M. (2004). Current science policies and their implications for the formation and maintenance of academic identity. *Higher Education Policy, 17*(2), 167. doi:10.1057/palgrave.hep.8300049

Hoffman, S. G. (2011). The new tools of the science trade: Contested knowledge production and the conceptual vocabularies of academic capitalism. *Social Anthropology, 19*(4), 439–462. doi:10.1111/j.1469-8676.2011.00180.x

Kantasalmi, K., & Tuunainen, J. (2018). Discipline-making and organizational permeability of the university: Discussing the notion of organizational field. *Research in the Sociology of Organizations, 57*, 331–359. doi:10.1108/S0733-558X20180000057013

Kogan, M. (2000). Higher education communities and academic identity. *Higher Education Quarterly, 54*(3), 207–216. doi:10.1111/1468-2273.00156

Latour, B. (1987). *Science in action: How to follow scientists and engineers through society*. Cambridge, MA: Harvard University Press.

Leydesdorff, L. (2012). The triple helix, quadruple helix, . . . and an N-tuple of helices: Explanatory models for analyzing the knowledge-based economy? *Journal of the Knowledge Economy, 3*(1), 25–35. doi:10.1007/s13132-011-0049-4

McNie, E. C. (2007). Reconciling the supply of scientific information with user demands: An analysis of the problem and review of the literature. *Environmental Science and Policy, 10*(1), 17–38. doi:10.1016/j.envsci.2006.10.004

Meagher, L., Lyall, C., & Nutley, S. (2008). Flows of knowledge, expertise and influence: A method for assessing policy and practice impacts from social science research. *Research Evaluation, 17*(3), 163–173. doi:10.3152/095820208X331720

Moore, R. (2013). *Basil Bernstein: The thinker and the field*. London: Routledge.

Nowotny, H., Scott, P., & Gibbons, M. (2003). Introduction: 'Mode 2' revisited: The new production of knowledge. *Minerva, 41*(3), 179–194. doi:10.1023/A%3A1025505528250

Papatsiba, V., & Cohen, E. (2020). Knowledge with impact in higher education research. In J. Huisman & M. Tight (Eds.), *Theory and method in higher education research (Theory and Method in Higher Education Research, Volume 6)*. Bingley: Emerald Publishing Limited. doi:10.1108/S2056-375220200000006013

Ponomariov, B., & Boardman, C. (2010). Influencing scientists' collaboration and productivity patterns through new institutions: University research centers and scientific and technical human capital. *Research Policy, 39*(5), 613–624. doi:10.1016/j.respol.2010.02.013

Putnam, L. L. (2009). Symbolic capital and academic fields. *Management Communication Quarterly, 23*(1), 127–134. doi:10.1177/0893318909335420

Royal Society. (2010). *The scientific century: Securing our future prosperity*. Retrieved from https://royalsociety.org/~/media/Royal_Society_Content/policy/publications/2010/4294970126.pdf

Schmidt, J. (2011). Toward an epistemology of nano-technosciences. *International Journal of Ethics of Science and Technology Assessment, 8*(2), 103–124. doi:10.1007/s10202-011-0104-z

Slaughter, S., Archerd, C. J., & Campbell, T. I. D. (2004). Boundaries and quandaries: How professors negotiate market relations. *Review of Higher Education, 28*(1), 129–165. doi:10.1353/rhe.2004.0032

Slaughter, S., Campbell, T., Holleman, M., & Morgan, E. (2002). The "traffic" in graduate students: Graduate students as tokens of exchange between academe and industry. *Science, Technology, & Human Values, 27*(2), 282–312. doi:10.1177/016224390202700205

Ternouth, P., Herrmann, K., & Docherty, D. (2010). *Absorbing research: The role of university research in business and market innovation*. Retrieved from www.rcuk.ac.uk/publications/reports/absorbingresearch/

Watermeyer, R. (2015). Lost in the 'third space': The impact of public engagement in higher education on academic identity, research practice and career progression. *European Journal of Higher Education, 5*(3), 1–17. doi:10.1080/21568235.2015.1044546

Watermeyer, R. (2016). Public intellectuals vs. new public management: The defeat of public engagement in higher education. *Studies in Higher Education, 41*(12), 2271–2285. doi:10.1080/03075079.2015.1034261

Wright, S. (2016). Universities in a knowledge economy or ecology? Policy, contestation and abjection. *Critical Policy Studies, 10*(1), 59–78. doi:10.1080/19460171.2016.1142457

Ziman, J. M. (1984). *An introduction to science studies: The philosophical and social aspects of science and technology*. Cambridge: Cambridge University Press.

Ziman, J. M. (1996a). Postacademic science: Constructing knowledge with networks and norms. *Science Studies, 9*(1), 67–80.

Ziman, J. M. (1996b). Science studies from pole to pole: A Hooker-Restivo connection? (Book review). *Minerva, 34*, 309–314.

5 The future of the university and its boundaries

Although parts of this short book have been data driven, the empirical analyses were included primarily to illustrate the conceptual tools developed, which centre around a Bernsteinian conceptualisation of the metaphor of social boundaries. The main theme throughout the conceptual and empirical sections of the book has been how academia enacts mechanisms to preserve relative power over its bounded domain of authority, that is, the production and transmission of society's (scientific) knowledge base, in large part by asserting control over its interactions with the wider society. Bernstein (2000) refers to this as 'regulating' boundaries. Regulation requires active effort and engagement across boundaries rather than a simplistic hardening and insulation of boundaries because the reproduction and enhancement of the academic enterprise requires not only that it maintain its distinctiveness, autonomy and boundedness, but also that these privileges are considered legitimate in wider society and this means engaging in boundary transactions in an 'exchange relationship' (Kogan, 2000, p. 215) with non-academic actors/organisations. Boundary transactions therefore emerged as key sites of activity which determine the development of academic boundaries, such as their weakening or reproduction.

In order to find instances of academic science likely to be rich in boundary transactions for study, I deliberately sampled programmes of research that had been recognised for their non-academic impacts in REF2014. This means that they are not likely to be representative of the whole academic sector. However, it also means that I have been able to focus my study on programmes of research that are likely to be highly influential and perhaps perceived of as models or 'ideals' of academic activity, not only in the United Kingdom where the study was conducted, but also in the vast number of other countries interested in the effect of United Kingdom's impact policies on the university sector.

Another emerging theme of the book, particularly the empirically driven chapters (3 and 4), has been sector variation. Despite sampling exclusively from STEMM disciplines and from 'high-impact' research, the variations that exist within academia have significantly shaped the narrative. Indeed, in an institution as complex and varied as the university, it would be unwise to expect all its dimensions, activities and missions to be on identical trajectories, even if they share many contexts and challenges (Clark, 1983). 'Wisdom, then, begins with the will to disaggregate, seeking to give proper weight to settings that make a difference' (Clark, 1987, p. xxii). My study has shown that it is only through a multidimensional analysis that the insights enabled by the boundary lens can be maximised, since academia does not consist of one single boundary, but rather is complexly contoured and non-uniform in its activities, priorities and boundedness. The key dimensions that I have analysed in this book are institutional status, research orientation and branch of science, each of which can mediate the interplays of power and control over academic boundaries and boundary transactions, therefore potentially creating different boundary trajectories for different segments of academia.

The first half of this final chapter details these variations and their implications, where necessary introducing new data not presented in Chapters 3 or 4. The second half of the chapter will summarise the value of the conceptual tools developed within the book for advancing analyses and debates pertaining to the interplays of power and control over academia's organisation and activities, also returning to the question of whether the university is an institution that is thriving or merely surviving.

Differentiated boundaries, different futures?

Institutional status

Not surprisingly given the stratified nature of the United Kingdom's higher education sector, departments in higher 'status' (Boliver, 2015) institutional contexts exhibited greater power and control over their boundaries and boundary transactions. One of the manifestations of this was the difference in how academics instigated external collaborations and sought users and support for their research. In most of the programmes of research I studied for this book, academics often went to significant effort and would engage in potentially costly boundary transactions in order to generate support and interest from potential sponsors and users, even though this could mean 'ceding some control' (Rosinger, Taylor, Coco, & Slaughter, 2016, p. 45) over the transactions and even, in some cases, over the research itself. Academics, at least at certain stages of a programme of research, would become more responsive and flexible to outside needs and interests (McNie, Parris, & Sarewitz, 2016) and show a greater willingness to adapt their activities and focus if necessary. Examples of this include departments setting up industry consortia or appointing industry or public sector scientists to leading academic posts so that these external actors and organisations are able to shape the department's research agenda and consolidate a department's relationship to important stakeholders, sponsors and user groups. In most cases then, academia's efforts to develop closer relationships with user groups involved ceding greater control over the terms of the relationship to these groups.

However, this was less often the case for those based in departments classified as 'elite' (see the sections on sampling in Chapter 2 and the Appendix). Interviewees based in 'elite' departments reported less effort required to generate support from users and that often they were being sought after themselves:

> We have a lot of industry supporters who are very keen to work with us. We don't have any trouble finding users.
>
> (Interviewee, 'elite' department)

> We've said [to the sector] . . . 'The onus is on you to come to us and give us the data to work with, because the more you put in, the more you get out'. And they all approach us, most of them want to be involved.
>
> (Interviewee, 'elite' department)

Similarly, most interviewees spoke about the difficulty of being able to generate and demonstrate 'REF-able' impact (i.e., likely to be acceptable to and successful in the REF) from their research and related boundary transactions. Attempts to generate such impact would take them into uncertain settings where they could not be sure about how they and their contributions would be or were received:

> Although you give them the evidence, you don't always know what they've really taken into account when they make their decisions, because there's different influences, not just the . . . research, but also political agendas.
>
> (Interviewee, 'less prestigious' department)

> With these [REF] Impact Case Studies, you have to try and demonstrate that you've actually changed something, then you get a big tick . . . but really [shrugs].
>
> (Interviewee, 'more prestigious' department)

But again, the respondents from 'elite' departments described very different experiences. Just as they did not seem to have to change in the ways that most other academics did in order to generate support and interest from users, they also did not seem to need to step so far out of their comfort zone in order to generate REF impact. This goes for 'elite' departments even from very different epistemic contexts:

> Most of what we did for this Impact Case Study, we probably would have done anyway. But because of the REF we were guided to do it in a more structured and organised manner. ... So although it doesn't sit very well with me philosophically, having to justify everything through impact, I think, practically, we can work with it. ... You have to work within the system and we're happy to do that.
>
> (Basic scientist, 'elite' department)

> Impact in the REF sense is not something I drive towards. It's more an academic hoop to jump through. But if all it takes is a bit of gathering and passing on information and that helps our impact in the REF, then brilliant.
>
> (Applied scientist, 'elite' department)

An analysis of the specific forms of boundary transaction across different institutional contexts also reveals 'elite' departments' relatively greater control and ownership over their boundary transactions. For example, in 'more' and 'less' prestigious departments, collaboration – a relatively costly form of transaction – is common (50% and 75% of cases, respectively), whereas 'elite' departments normally avoid this more costly transaction (only 25% of cases) (see Figure 5.1). Collaboration is costly because it implies ceding ownership over the production of academic knowledge to non-academic actors. By contrast, user-oriented outputs – less costly because they allow

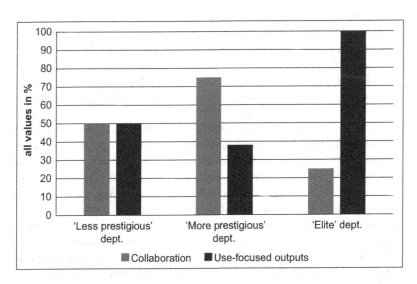

Figure 5.1 Bar chart showing forms of transaction by departmental status

the academics far more ownership over production and content – is apparent in all research sampled from 'elite' departments but only 50% and 38%, respectively, of that from 'more' and 'less prestigious' departments.

Adopting a similar Bernsteinian 'boundary' lens to myself, Mary Douglas (1996) – a close intellectual colleague of Bernstein's – suggests that where a group is sufficiently powerful and bounded, it may be less 'exposed to the need to communicate with outsiders' (Douglas, 1996, p. 55). In other words, more powerfully bounded categories or groups have greater power over their boundaries and more regulatory control over their boundary transactions. This means that more powerful universities at the top of the academic 'hierarchy' will likely be better able to insulate themselves from 'the *exigencies of the market*' (Bernstein, 2000, p. 60, original emphasis). My own research finds that powerful institutional contexts are associated with greater ability to resist pressures to engage in boundary transactions which disagree with their own sense of what is appropriate or valuable; they will tend to engage in boundary transactions which do not challenge their ownership or control over academic knowledge, which allow them to enact and reinforce their distinctive relation to knowledge and which incur relatively few costs. By contrast, less powerful institutional contexts are associated with more costly boundary transactions which may pose greater challenges to their academic identity, autonomy, authority and values.

Research orientation

Chapters 3 and 4 have already included some discussion of differences between disciplinary research orientations, particularly the contrasts that my study revealed between applied and basic disciplines. In this section, I synthesise the relevant findings to highlight the meanings and implications of different research orientations for academic boundaries and boundary transactions, also bringing into the discussion the third category of research orientation, 'use-inspired basic' research.

To briefly recap and reframe some findings from Chapter 3, my analysis found that the boundary transactions of basic science tend to do more to contribute to the reinforcement of academic boundaries than those of applied science. For instance, nearly all cases of basic sciences involved opportunities for students to act as 'boundary-spanners' in ways that advanced not only the research and its impact, but also students' own training and employability, thereby allowing the academic department to contribute to its third missions and its own distinctive core missions (research and teaching) simultaneously. By contrast, fewer than half of the cases sampled from applied or use-inspired basic disciplines involved such opportunities. Similarly, basic sciences were often able to generate new technologies which had the joint function of advancing their own academic research while also benefiting non-academic users, again enabling the department to simultaneously advance its third mission and core research mission. By contrast, the user-oriented outputs from applied sciences rarely fed back into the research process in this way.

In comparing basic and applied sciences, then, my study does not necessarily find that basic sciences are more 'closed off' or 'insulated' than applied sciences; as Chapter 4 showed, both basic and applied science could become deeply intertwined with non-academic systems of scientific and technological application. Rather, the main difference lies in the ability of basic sciences, in the process of conducting boundary-crossing transactions, to simultaneously contribute to core academic missions. This allows the departments to enact their distinctive values to wider society in ways which simultaneously enact and assert their own distinctive internal values.

It might be expected that use-inspired basic disciplines would exhibit practices and processes that simply fall somewhere in between those of basic and applied disciplines. However, my analysis found that use-inspired basic research was in some ways even more 'bounded' than basic research. To be sure, academics in use-inspired basic disciplines were often highly motivated by the goal of achieving non-academic impact through their research. But what distinguished use-inspired basic science, particularly from applied scientists, was the long-term and knowledge-focused nature of such goals, which could often mean having periods of research which is relatively 'unapplied' (see the following quote) and instead focused on advancing fundamental knowledge:

> I've been working on this since 2002 and for the first several years of that it was very unapplied.
> (Use-inspired basic scientist)

> When I first did my study here I did more like a lab-based study, and I was thinking, okay, it's an 'applied' area, and I might get a 'significant result', but in terms of impact, is that really making a difference in everyday life?
> (Use-inspired basic scientist)

However, spending at least some time on 'unapplied' stages of research was often considered important because use-inspired basic research meant not merely focusing on short-term, localised solutions but, crucially, developing the theoretical scope and understanding of the *discipline*. What sets much of the use-inspired research in my sample apart, then, is the way in which its impact mission is so bound up with the more traditionally academic objective of advancing an academic discipline; in other words, the discipline itself becomes a direct and necessary (although not always sufficient) vehicle through which to achieve use-inspired goals.

The data reveals some interesting illustrations of this distinctive feature of use-inspired basic research. For example, interviewees from use-inspired basic disciplines were the only ones in my sample to bring up the role and importance of theory, and when they did so, they highlighted the links between theory and impact:

> Whether it's teaching, training, consultancy, research, whatever, I'm working with theory, but at the same time always thinking how to make sure the theory is relevant. The transfer from theory to practice and the links between theory and practice, as well as to policy, are really important to me.
>
> (Use-inspired basic scientist)

> My theoretical background . . . was originally quite abstract and very scientific. . . . Now, I still work theoretically, but I've made the decision to use the theory but to be driven by practical goals.
>
> (Use-inspired basic scientist)

Another example is the use of 'bridging concepts' as a form of boundary transaction. As explained in Chapter 3, these are concepts which condense underpinning scientific research and theory into a more readily understandable concept so as to be suitable for consideration and application by non-specialist users and stakeholders. Although I identified only three clear cases of such bridging concepts in my study, two of these were from use-inspired disciplines of psychopharmacology and environmental science (the third being from the applied science of civil engineering).

Through such use-inspired basic research, academia is able to internalise objects of the world that are of most pressing interest and relevance to non-academic society precisely by internalising them into that most academic of organisational forms: the academic discipline. In a sense, use-inspired basic disciplines are themselves a form of boundary transaction (i.e., a 'boundary structure') and this achieves a situation whereby the enactment and advancement of academia's 'third' or 'impact' missions become virtually synonymous with the advancement of its own sui generis institutional identity (Durkheim, 2013; see also Chapter 4). Although not without risk, use-inspired basic science therefore arguably represents the most promising research orientation from the perspective of academia's attempt to regulate and reinforce its boundaries in the context of the impact agenda and the knowledge society.

Branch of science

In Chapter 4, I discussed how academia's 'production' of significant numbers of doctoral graduates, who then enter non-academic sectors, functions as a key mechanism through which academia regulates its boundaries, because it serves to fundamentally change the external environment, or knowledge 'ecology', in ways that lower the costs of transacting with these key sectors. However, I also found that this appeared to benefit some disciplines more than others in my sample, particularly those associated with the formal sciences, and less so those associated with the life sciences. As Figure 5.2 shows, less than 20% of the cases sampled from formal science departments were found to bring academics into interactions with non-doctorate holders. By contrast, most (nearly 60%) cases of life science in my study involve interacting with at least one if not several non-PhD holders. Lastly, sitting in between the life and formal sciences, natural science involves interactions with non-doctorate holders in approximately 40% of cases. In other words, formal scientists are often able to limit their transactions with non-academics with whom they share a strong epistemic background, therefore benefiting most from the reduced transaction costs that this allows.

Interview data revealed these benefits. Generally, formal scientists experienced far simpler transactions, with some explicitly expressing awareness

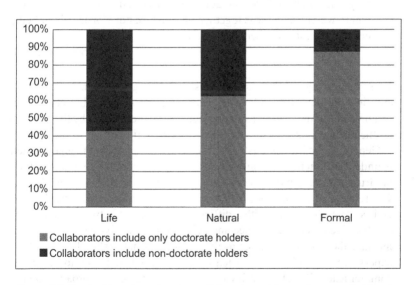

Figure 5.2 Stacked bar chart showing collaboration with non-doctorate holders by branch of science

about the benefits of being able to focus their external collaborations with doctoral graduates. For example:

> Most if not all of the particular group that we worked with had PhDs and many will have ongoing links with different university departments, so they would understand the research environment of a university and the mode of operation if you like.
>
> (Formal scientist)

Experiences of other formal scientists interviewed corroborate this point and highlight their relatively trouble-free experience of transacting across boundaries, even when working with the private sector where the ultimate goal of generating profits could potentially bring collaborators into conflict:

> I think the technical challenges of working with industry are manageable, the personal challenges are manageable. I don't find any issues.
>
> (Formal scientist)

> We work with a lot of companies all in the same sector . . . and it is competitive because they're trying to guard what they've got. But when we work with them, we're working typically with the companies' engineers, not the managers or the accountants or what have you, and they [the engineers] have all got similar needs and we provide a forum where we all share ideas together, and they're not worried about being competitive, it's an open discussion.
>
> (Formal scientist)

These quotes suggest that a shared epistemic background can overcome not only institutional barriers between academia and industry, but also, under certain conditions (in this case, conditions that were enabled by the academics themselves), barriers between industry competitors.

Generally, the life scientists faced significantly greater challenges in their boundary transactions, mainly citing issues around building and maintaining trust with external partners and stakeholders. As discussed in Chapter 4 in relation to the analysis of individual-level academic identity, life scientists were often faced with a difficult balancing act between maintaining an objective and neutral stance and being more proactive in terms of arguing that the science suggests a given policy. What makes life scientists' experience so challenging in such circumstances is the need to be able to communicate difficult scientific concepts and realities to a broad audience. Some of my interviewees reflected on engaging with various policy and community actors:

> I have to work with a lot of policy people, government employees, NGOs [non-governmental organisations], and some of these people are very naïve when it comes to the implications of these scientific issues. But I have to find a language which reduces some of this complexity and package it for them logically so that they can learn. . . . But it's no surprise they find it difficult because it quickly gets quite technical . . . even some of us are a bit hazy on some of it sometimes.
>
> (Life scientist)

> It's really hard to explain this stuff, most people just don't understand it. . . . So that's a challenge. I wouldn't say we've overcome it but that's why we've got to keep communicating as well as we can all the time.
>
> (Life scientist)

Others also spoke of similar challenges when communicating their research via the media:

> The way the media want you to give a message is very black and white, but in science it's never black and white. . . . They want to know – *'Is it dangerous or not? Is it worse or better . . . ?'* But 'worse' in terms of what? . . . As a scientist it is difficult to give a message that is accurate because the media just wants to turn it into headlines.
>
> (Life scientist)

> The media are always happy to run with anything on these kinds of topics, . . . the good news and the bad news. One of our papers made the front page and the headline referred to a 'miracle'. . . . [But it has] also been constantly in the press with . . . suggestions of all sorts of negative things as well.
>
> (Life scientist)

To draw on Bernstein's (2000) concepts, researchers in the formal sciences are able to communicate via 'restricted' code – a shortened, 'intimate and immediate' (Moore, 2013, pp. 66–67) form of communication exhibited within a group of people who can take for granted a significant amount of shared prior knowledge and understanding. By contrast, researchers in other branches of science must more frequently communicate using 'elaborating' code (Bernstein, 2000; Moore, 2013), which is more intensive and costly.

But despite these variations, the branch of science emerged as less of a factor than institutional status and research orientation in shaping and mediating academics' engagement in boundary transactions. In this, I agree with other recent research which suggests that relatively more weight should be attached to the culture, mission and expectations of the particular university to which an academic belongs than to one's academic discipline (Shields & Watermeyer, 2020). Trowler (2014) too has, partly through adoption of a Bernsteinian sociological lens, recently advanced his theoretical depiction of academic disciplines as fixed 'tribes' to a more 'nuanced' analysis in which disciplines are only partially and contingently causal structures, operating 'in dynamic combination with other structural phenomena' (pp. 1722, 1728).

The twenty-first-century university through the boundary lens

This book has developed and applied conceptual tools to inform debates, analyses and possibilities for the university, particularly academic research, centred around a sociological conceptualisation of the 'boundary' metaphor. The boundary metaphor has been well used in the sociologies of knowledge, higher education, science and organisation and, by way of the theoretical legacy of Basil Bernstein, I have harnessed this literature to develop a 'boundary lens' through which to focus on key interplays of 'power' and 'control' (Bernstein, 2000) over academic organisation, activities and relations and to assess the state of academic boundaries and academia's capacity to define and control these boundaries.

In one of the more incisive applications of the boundary metaphor, Considine (2006) challenges the sector to reflect on and develop a 'boundary-creating self-conception for the university' (p. 269), in other words, to define the terms on which academic boundaries may be shaped, crossed and maintained. One influential self-conception that has been proposed for the twenty-first-century university is the conception of the 'entrepreneurial university' as described and, to an extent, promoted by Clark (1998, 2004a, 2004b) and Etzkowitz (1983, 2009, 2013). Although prescribing caution about 'the leap too far . . . over traditional academic boundaries' (Clark, 2004b, p. 78), Clark (2004a) pointed optimistically forward to a twenty-first-century university that would institute 'a state of continuous change' in order to respond and 'adapt effectively to a changing society' and which would combine competition and revenue generation with a tolerance for 'cross-subsidizing . . . "useless" things' so as to contribute to the 'cultivation and transmission of a cultural heritage as well as to economic progress' (pp. 357–358). Etzkowitz and Viale (2010) summarised the situation for academic boundaries in the entrepreneurial university as follows:

> Bounded entities persist but the boundaries are permeable; with networks and collaborations giving organizations an outward as well as an inward focus. Networking and taking advantage of complementarities

supersedes 'boundary work', or defence of structures, as an organizational priority.

(Etzkowitz & Viale, 2010, p. 602)

The entrepreneurial university is therefore presented as an institution which has found a way to absorb the forces being exerted on it from powerful external institutions and turn these forces into opportunities to advance its own position. Shields and Watermeyer (2020) have written similarly of the 'paradox' of the university, arguing that, at least in theory, the paradox may become a 'source of stability' (p. 13) and therefore a source of its own resolution. The entrepreneurial university promises just such a resolution to the paradox of the university as seen through the boundary lens – that to thrive it must cross boundaries and be engaged in an increasingly complex, multidimensional and knowledge-intensive society, but that to survive means simultaneously reinforcing the integrity of its own boundaries and boundedness. This promised resolution would take the form of a 'stability' (Shields & Watermeyer, 2020, p. 13) whereby the reproduction of academia and its boundaries is achieved through a (relatively regulated) series of boundary transactions.

My own analysis does, to an extent, align with Etzkowitz and Viale's (2010) view. I have shown that boundary transactions can act as mechanisms through which academia regulates its boundaries at the same time as it enacts and enhances its value to and role within wider society. The programmes of research sampled in my study were found to exhibit multiple forms of boundary transaction and multiple mechanisms for effectively regulating academic boundaries in this way. The empirical parts of this book, and the data on which they are based, are replete with effective ways to minimise the costs and maximise the gains of boundary transactions – seemingly prerequisites if academia is going to thrive in the twenty-first-century knowledge society.

However, my analysis also gives reason to be cautious about concluding that genuine stability has been achieved. The boundary lens allowed me to reveal significant variations in a dataset that could at face value have been quite homogeneous, with all sampled programmes of research having been selected on the basis of being 'high-impact' and STEMM-based. The revealed variations underscore both the different ways in which powerful external institutions are exerting control over academia's boundary transactions and the different capacities of different sections of academia to mediate these external powers and exert their own control. One example, albeit with perhaps only moderate implications for different capacities to manage boundaries and boundary transactions, was that formal scientists were more frequently able to engage in low-cost transactions, while natural scientists and, even more so, life scientists often engaged in more costly forms of transaction. Somewhat more significantly, I found evidence of research in applied sciences shifting towards what Ziman (1996) saw as a 'post-academic' science system, as certain academic fields become increasingly embedded within a market-oriented Mode 2 knowledge production system governed by economic interests. Not that basic sciences were exempt from external powers; their research was found to be relatively more influenced by more obvious 'powers', such as those associated with national security and defence that see advances in the research capabilities of basic sciences as a means to ensure technoscientific power. But in the process, basic sciences also maintained more distinctively 'academic' characteristics than that observable in the applied sciences. Most consequentially of all, I argue, institutional 'status' or 'prestige' was found to be significantly associated with control over boundary transactions. My study suggests that 'higher status' departments will be better able to avoid the greatest external pressures facing the sector and to engage in boundary transactions which do not challenge their ownership or control over academic knowledge or sense of academic identity. By contrast, those departmental contexts less able to secure resources and prestige according to traditional academic criteria will be more 'exposed' (Douglas, 1996, p. 55) to the need to engage in those riskier and costlier transactions demanded by external sources of power, over which academics are likely to have less control.

Barnett (2017), with the benefit of nearly two decades' hindsight of the twenty-first century and the challenges it poses for the university, has urged a new self-conception for the university which he presents 'as a contender with that of the entrepreneurial university' (p. 171), namely the 'ecological university'. The ecological university sees its 'self-reproduction' and 'self-interest' (Barnett, 2017, p. 47) as dependent on something more than just an 'exchange relationship' (Kogan, 2000, p. 215). The ecological university, instead, demands 'reciprocity' (Barnett, 2017, p. 152). The implication of this focus on reciprocity is that the ecological university is fundamentally aware of external 'institutions which are imbued with power . . . [and] forces that are destabilizing the university and steering it in certain pernicious directions', and is thus motivated to proactively 'maintain . . . its own locus, giving neither the political nor the economic institutions simply what they call for' (Barnett, 2017, pp. 159, 171).

Barnett (2017) invokes Bernstein to argue against a university motivated solely by hardening boundaries and for a more positive approach to 'boundary maintenance' (p. 47) which involves frequent (albeit regulated) 'boundary crossing' (p. 51) and which 'is never content to reside within its own present boundaries – of knowledge, academic identity, understandings, position, relationships with the world or pedagogical relationships' (p. 78).

But Barnett does not see today's model of boundary-crossing universities as institutions that are enjoying a state of stability. Rather, he argues that much in contemporary academic policy and culture, particularly the impact agenda, is undermining the 'reciprocity' (Barnett, 2017, p. 145) that is so crucial to effective, authentic and sustainable boundary transactions in his 'ecological' conception: 'Impact has no time for reciprocity. . . . It conjures an *instrumental* form of engagement . . . a connectivity that is devoid of a relationship. . . . It is evident that the language of impact has to be not merely abandoned, but sharply repudiated' (Barnett, 2017, pp. 144–145, original emphasis). Although writing before the emergence of an explicit discourse of impact, Bernstein (2000) critiqued the REF's predecessor system, the Research Assessment Exercise, as well as the associated systemic culture of which it was not just a part, but a major driving force in the UK context. For Bernstein (2000), such systems risk being guilty of 'misrecognition', that is, they are grounded on a 'generic' and narrowly '*functional* analysis' (p. 53, emphasis added) about the value of academic work, as if its value could be captured in some simplistic measure of 'productivity' in terms of 'narrow, short-term inputs and outputs' (Rhoades, 2001, p. 620). Such systems threaten to reduce academic work to a mere 'performance . . . of what is taken to be . . . necessary' (Bernstein, 2000, p. 53) to the achievement of the generic goal of producing quantifiable 'outputs'.

In the context of the REF and the impact agenda, then, the danger is that we are allowing a culture which misrecognises what is distinctive, and distinctively valuable, about academia, including the reality that academia's sui generis (Durkheim, 2013) identity and trajectory is already fundamentally geared towards research and other activities that authentically engage with and contribute to the 'real world'. That this is so is evidenced, for example, by my analysis of use-inspired basic disciplines as emerging organically from academic forms of inquiry, and by the fact that most of the programmes of research sampled for my study were use- or 'impact'-oriented long before the impact agenda crystallised into an area of assessment in the REF (see also Watermeyer, 2012). To the extent that the impact agenda promotes merely the insincere 'performance' of impact, as if impact is achieved merely by compliance with regulatory and assessment systems or abstracted 'best practices', it risks misrecognising and potentially stifling and undermining these authentic user-orientations of academics, pointing them towards inauthentic claims of impact rather than more meaningful long-term goals grounded in authentic academic motivations (Chubb & Watermeyer, 2017; Watermeyer, 2019; Watermeyer & Hedgecoe, 2016). It is telling that my own interview respondents – despite most of them being deeply passionate about benefiting the world through their research, despite some stating that the inclusion of 'impact' in the REF had increased the status of and support for their research and despite all having benefited professionally from producing highly rated REF impact case studies – spoke critically of REF impact in general, perhaps implicitly recognising the misrecognition inherent in the REF. My participants spoke of REF impact as placing unnecessary administrative burdens on universities and their staff and inappropriate expectations on many fields of research; most participants felt that their own topics of research and approaches to engaging potential collaborators and users 'just so happened' to coincide with what was valued in REF2014, but none, when asked, felt that this was something that all researchers and research fields should be expected to aim for or be evaluated on.

Perhaps particularly but by no means exclusively in the United Kingdom, the focus on using the expertise and outputs of the bounded institution of academia to generate benefits for actors and organisations beyond academic boundaries has given rise to a situation in which there is such pressure on increasing the frequencies and intensities of boundary transactions that they threaten the very boundaries within which academia's expertise is nurtured and in which academic outputs are given the space and insulation that their development often requires. And yet, as I have argued throughout this book, closing off academic boundaries is not a viable response. The reality that boundary transactions can neither be fully avoided nor be allowed to proceed unregulated, and that attempts to thrive may bring universities face-to-face with potential threats to survival, are necessary tensions that are fundamental to the fulfilment and enactment of the academic enterprise itself. Although they present difficult and ongoing challenges for academia, acknowledging the necessity and permanence of these tensions may also be liberating because it highlights that any specific manifestation of these tensions are only temporary. For example, the impact agenda, including its institutionalisation in the United Kingdom's REF, is a non-necessary manifestation of necessary tensions, and as such can and should be challenged and resisted on grounds of protecting the long-term reproduction of academia as a distinct and distinctly valuable institution. The realisation is both liberating and challenging because it puts the onus to ensure academia's positive and constructive engagement with and contribution to society squarely on those of us who work within and care about academia.

The fact that my sampled departments and programmes of research exhibited notable power and control over their boundaries and boundary transactions may well be a selection effect, given that I sampled research that was highly rated in the REF. This was a useful sampling decision in the context of my small-scale empirical study as it allowed me to easily identify research rich in boundary transactions and cost-lowering mechanisms and to focus on the kinds of STEMM research and boundary transactions that may become the model for those wanting to replicate REF success. It also allowed me to explore other variables more deeply and thereby reveal potentially different trajectories associated with different academic contexts, including contexts associated with lower capacity for exerting power and control over boundaries and boundary transactions, the most significant being, at least in stratified systems like the United Kingdom, those institutional contexts with a relatively lower position in the hierarchy. However, as interplays of power and control over universities in the twenty-first century have so far functioned to 'repurpose' academic activity and 'reshape' academic boundaries (Wright, 2016, pp. 61, 71) according to external criteria of powerful political and economic institutions, it is important that the boundary lens is used to focus on broader samples of academic research and related activity, including contexts less likely to have the capacity to regulate or control their boundaries and transactions. My study has shown the mechanisms through which academia can continue to transact across boundaries whilst also regulating and reproducing its boundaries, but the reproduction of academic boundaries in the twenty-first century remains contested and contingent rather than guaranteed. As such, a focus on the 'least powerful' sections of academia is important not just in order to generate critical analyses of academic hierarchies, but also because they may show the earliest signs of the weakening of academic boundaries and the ceding of control over boundary transactions. Ongoing application of the boundary lens in general will therefore contribute to ongoing analyses of the academic sector and keep track of whether academia is thriving – reproducing its boundaries whilst crossing them to contribute to and provide value to a reciprocal knowledge ecology – or barely surviving – caught between the need to justify itself to and to protect itself from other powerful sectors of society.

References

Barnett, R. (2017). *The ecological university: A feasible utopia*. London: Routledge.
Bernstein, B. (2000). *Pedagogy, symbolic control, and identity: Theory, research, critique* (2nd ed.). Oxford: Rowman & Littlefield.
Boliver, V. (2015). Are there distinctive clusters of higher and lower status universities in the UK? *Oxford Review of Education*, *41*(5), 608–627. doi:10.1080/0305 4985.2015.1082905
Chubb, J., & Watermeyer, R. (2017). Artifice or integrity in the marketization of research impact? Investigating the moral economy of (pathways to) impact statements within research funding proposals in the UK and Australia. *Studies in Higher Education*, *42*(12), 2360–2372. doi:10.1080/03075079.2016.1144182
Clark, B. R. (1983). *The higher education system: Academic organisation in cross-national perspective*. London: University of California Press.

Clark, B. R. (1987). *The academic life: Small worlds, different worlds*. A Carnegie Foundation Special Report (0931050324). Retrieved from https://eric.ed.gov/?id=ED299902

Clark, B. R. (1998). *Creating entrepreneurial universities: Organizational pathways of transformation*. Oxford: Pergamon Press.

Clark, B. R. (2004a). Delineating the character of the entrepreneurial university. *Higher Education Policy, 17*(4), 355. doi:10.1057/palgrave.hep.8300062

Clark, B. R. (2004b). *Sustaining change in universities: Continuities in case studies and concepts*. Maidenhead: Open University Press.

Considine, M. (2006). Theorizing the university as a cultural system: Distinctions, identities, emergencies. *Educational Theory, 56*(3), 255–270. doi:10.1111/j.1741-5446.2006.00231.x

Douglas, M. (1996). *Natural symbols: Explorations in cosmology*. London: Routledge.

Durkheim, É. (2013). *The evolution of educational thought: Lectures on the formation and development of secondary education in France*. Oxon: Routledge.

Etzkowitz, H. (1983). Entrepreneurial scientists and entrepreneurial universities in American academic science. *A Review of Science, Learning and Policy, 21*(2), 198–233. doi:10.1007/BF01097964

Etzkowitz, H. (2009). Normative change in science: From entrepreneurial science to social entrepreneurship. In G. D. Libecap (Ed.), *Measuring the social value of innovation: A link in the university technology transfer and entrepreneurship equation* (Vol. 19). Bingley: Emerald Group Publishing Limited. doi:10.1108/S1048-4736(2009)0000019002

Etzkowitz, H. (2013). Anatomy of the entrepreneurial university. *Social Science Information, 52*(3), 486–511. doi:10.1177/0539018413485832

Etzkowitz, H., & Viale, R. (2010). Polyvalent knowledge and the entrepreneurial university: A third academic revolution? *Critical Sociology, 36*(4), 595–609. doi:10.1177/0896920510365921

Kogan, M. (2000). Higher education communities and academic identity. *Higher Education Quarterly, 54*(3), 207–216. doi:10.1111/1468-2273.00156

McNie, E. C., Parris, A., & Sarewitz, D. (2016). Improving the public value of science: A typology to inform discussion, design and implementation of research. *Research Policy, 45*(4), 884–895. doi:10.1016/j.respol.2016.01.004

Moore, R. (2013). *Basil Bernstein: The thinker and the field*. London: Routledge.

Rhoades, G. (2001). Managing productivity in an academic institution: Rethinking the whom, which, what, and whose of productivity. *Research in Higher Education, 42*(5), 619–632. doi:10.1023/A:1011006511651

Rosinger, K. O., Taylor, B. J., Coco, L., & Slaughter, S. (2016). Organizational segmentation and the prestige economy: Deprofessionalization in high- and low-resource departments. *The Journal of Higher Education, 87*(1), 27–54. doi:10.1080/00221546.2016.11777393

Shields, R., & Watermeyer, R. (2020). Competing institutional logics in universities in the United Kingdom: Schism in the church of reason. *Studies in Higher Education, 45*(1), 3–17. doi:10.1080/03075079.2018.1504910

Trowler, P. (2014). Depicting and researching disciplines: Strong and moderate essentialist approaches. *Studies in Higher Education, 39*(10), 1720–1731. doi:10.1080/03075079.2013.801431

Watermeyer, R. (2012). From engagement to impact? Articulating the public value of academic research. *Tertiary Education and Management, 18*(2), 115–130. doi:10.1080/13583883.2011.641578

Watermeyer, R. (2019). *Competitive accountability in academic life: The struggle for social impact and public legitimacy*. Cheltenham: Edward Elgar Publishing.

Watermeyer, R., & Hedgecoe, A. (2016). Selling 'impact': Peer reviewer projections of what is needed and what counts in REF impact case studies. A retrospective analysis. *Journal of Education Policy, 31*(5), 651–665. doi:10.1080/02680939.2016.1170885

Wright, S. (2016). Universities in a knowledge economy or ecology? Policy, contestation and abjection. *Critical Policy Studies, 10*(1), 59–78. doi:10.1080/19460171.2016.1142457

Ziman, J. M. (1996). Postacademic science: Constructing knowledge with networks and norms. *Science Studies, 9*(1), 67–80.

Appendix

Sampling 'impactful' research

Since I sampled cases of academic research from those which achieved a high 'Impact' rating in REF2014, I will briefly describe the REF2014 process and how it was possible to draw from it in my sampling strategy.

Within REF2014, research was assessed at the departmental (rather than university) level. Departments made their submissions to one of 36 disciplinary groupings, referred to as Units of Assessment (UoA). The 'impact' strand of the assessment requires departments to submit Impact Case Studies – the amount of Case Studies depends on the size of the department, but there is a minimum of two Case Studies per submission. Impact Case Studies are four-page narrative documents which describe a body of research with references to relevant research outputs, and which detail and evidence specific impacts resulting from that research. The descriptions and evidence of research outputs are provided in order to demonstrate how the submitting department's contributions were crucial to the impact. The judgement is based on the 'reach' and 'significance' of the non-academic impact which resulted from research, with the official definition of impact being 'an effect on, change or benefit to the economy, society, culture, public policy or services, health, the environment or quality of life, beyond academia' (Higher Education Funding Council for England, 2009). According to the official website (Research Excellence Framework 2014, 2014), Impact Case Studies are given a rating of between 1* to 4*, with the following definitions:

- 4* Impact: 'Outstanding impacts in terms of their reach and significance'.
- 3* Impact: 'Very considerable impacts in terms of their reach and significance'.
- 2* Impact: 'Considerable impacts in terms of their reach and significance'.
- 1* Impact: 'Recognised but modest impacts in terms of their reach and significance'.

Unclassified: 'The impact is of little or no reach and significance; or the impact was not eligible; or the impact was not underpinned by excellent research produced by the submitted unit'.

I sampled only research which contributed to 3* or 4* rated Case Studies, as I wanted my analysis to be able to shed light on the practices and processes associated with the kind of research being privileged in the current policy context (Laing, Mazzoli Smith, & Todd, 2018). REF2014 results are available at ref.ac.uk/2014. Note that although the website aggregates results to the level of departmental submissions, rather than individual Case Studies, it is possible to identify Case Studies which achieved either 3* or 4* by only sampling from departments which achieved 100% 3* or 4* ratings.

Classifying departments by prestige/status

Departments were classified into three institutional contexts: 'elite', 'more prestigious' and 'less prestigious'. There are two aspects of *institutional context* contributing to these departmental classifications: university status and departmental ranking. Regarding institutional status, I drew from Boliver's (2015) recent work. Her cluster analysis results in a four-tier structure of UK academic hierarchy: an elite Tier 1 includes only two institutions; Tier 2 comprises 39 institutions; Tier 3 is the largest, including 67 institutions; last, there is a small cluster of 19 institutions which make up Tier 4 (Boliver, 2015, pp. 619–620). My sample strategy targeted departments based in universities from all four clusters/tiers.

Next, regarding departmental ranking, I identify departments whose Overall REF2014 rating was relatively 'high', 'middle' and 'low' in relation to others within the same UoA. I ascertained these rankings from the Times Higher Education's (2014) publication of institutions ranked by UoA performance. Based on this, the submissions in my sample which I characterise as 'High' rank between 1st and 6th in their respective UoAs, while those characterised as 'Medium' rank between 9th and 28th, and those as 'Low' from between 37th and 40th.

Drawing from these sources then, the classifications are defined as follows:

- 'Elite' = (i) based in a Tier 1 or Tier 2 institution *and* (ii) having a 'high' overall rating in REF2014
- 'More prestigious' = *either*
    - (i) based in a Tier 1 or Tier 2 institution *but not* (ii) having a 'high' overall rating in REF2014, *or*

- (i) based in a Tier 3 or Tier 4 institution *but not* (ii) having a 'low' overall rating in REF2014
- 'Less prestigious' = (i) based in a Tier 3 or Tier 4 institution *and* (ii) having a 'low' overall rating in REF2014

Data collection

My initial approach to accessing documentary data was via an interactive online database of searchable and downloadable REF Impact Case Studies, which is accessible via the REF website (https://impact.ref.ac.uk/casestudies), an output of the commissioned work by King's College London and Digital Science (2015). I used the Impact Case Studies as a starting point and then followed up on various leads from there, including reading the research outputs referenced therein, and searching web-based material about the individuals and organisations involved in the research and its impact. I acknowledge Atkinson and Coffey's (2004) caution that documents are representations of 'a particular kind of documentary reality' (p. 61). Such documents as produced in the context of 'audit exercises like the RAE [Research Assessment Exercise, the REF's predecessor] . . . are intended to reflect the *coherence* of a department's research strategic thinking and the *cogency* of its research plans' (Atkinson & Coffey, 2004, p. 70, emphasis added), rather than the more complex and 'messier' aspects of the reality of academic research. I therefore emphasise that I treated these documents (and indeed all documents) with due caution. My main uses of the REF documents were to obtain a broad overview of the underpinning research and to identify the key academic and non-academic actors and organisational structures associated with the research. Overall, Impact Case Studies constituted only 8% of the documents studied, so my analysis was informed by a far broader set of documents, each of which I treated as representing only partial reality. Such documentary-led approaches, although still in a minority, are becoming more common in higher education research (Brennan, Papatsiba, Sousa, & Hoffman, 2016).

I aimed to interview one individual from each of the 19 sampled programmes of research. However, I was only able to secure participation for 14 of the 19 programmes of research (achieved through ten interviews, with some interviewees having participated in more than one programme of research). The ten interviews yielded over 11 hours of recorded data. Having drawn my data mainly from documentary sources, the interviews served to 'provide additional information that [may have been] missed' in my documentary searches, and 'to check the accuracy' of my interpretations (Maxwell, 2013, p. 103).

References

Atkinson, P., & Coffey, A. (2004). Analysing documentary realities. In D. Silverman (Ed.), *Qualitative research: Theory, method and practice* (2nd ed.). London: Sage.

Boliver, V. (2015). Are there distinctive clusters of higher and lower status universities in the UK? *Oxford Review of Education, 41*(5), 608–627. doi:10.1080/0305 4985.2015.1082905

Brennan, J., Papatsiba, V., Sousa, S. B., & Hoffman, D. (2016). Diversity of higher education institutions in networked knowledge societies: A comparative examination. In D. M. Hoffman & J. Välimaa (Eds.), *Re-becoming universities?: Higher education institutions in networked knowledge societies*. Dordrecht: Springer.

Higher Education Funding Council for England. (2009). *Research Excellence Framework: Second consultation on the assessment and funding of research*. Retrieved from http://dera.ioe.ac.uk/9288/

King's College London & Digital Science. (2015). *The nature, scale and beneficiaries of research impact: An initial analysis of Research Excellence Framework (REF) 2014 Impact Case Studies*. Retrieved from www.kcl.ac.uk/sspp/policy-institute/publications/Analysis-of-REF-impact.pdf

Laing, K., Mazzoli Smith, L., & Todd, L. (2018). The impact agenda and critical social research in education: Hitting the target but missing the spot? *Policy Futures in Education, 16*(2), 169–184. doi:10.1177/1478210317742214

Maxwell, J. A. (2013). *Qualitative research design: An interactive approach* (3rd ed.). Los Angeles: Sage.

Research Excellence Framework 2014. (2014). *Assessment criteria and level definitions*. Retrieved from www.ref.ac.uk/2014/panels/assessmentcriteriaandleveldefinitions/

Times Higher Education. (2014). Research Excellence Framework 2014: Institutions ranked by subject. Retrieved from www.timeshighereducation.com/sites/default/files/Attachments/2014/12/17/g/o/l/sub-14-01.pdf

Index

academic autonomy 1–4, 7, 51, 80, 84
academic capitalism 21, 23
academic careers 25, 53, 59, 71
academic freedom 1, 6, 68
academic hierarchy 9, 84, 95, 99
academic identity: enactment 42, 51, 57, 61, 72, 85; individual level 4, 44, 46–48, 51, 54, 68–73, 88; institutional level 1–2, 6–9, 17–19, 61, 65–68, 86, 92–93
academic legitimacy: external 5–7, 16, 19, 48, 51, 58, 80; internal 3, 27, 47, 68; undermining of 23, 48, 63, 72
academic management 1, 3, 7, 24
academic mobility 25, 59–60, 64
academic values 3, 21, 34, 57, 61; alignment of 17, 31, 46, 54, 65, 75; challenges to 1, 4, 23, 42, 69–70, 84; distinctiveness of 7, 30, 51, 66, 73, 85
applied research 32, 92; *see also* research, orientation

Barnett, Ron 92–93
basic research 21, 48, 54–55, 92; *see also* research, orientation
Beck, John 71
Bernstein, Basil 5, 27, 80, 84, 89–90, 92–93; and control 16–18, 42, 51, 57, 63–64, 66, 94–95; and power 14–16, 18, 71, 94–95
biology 29, 45, 48, 55, 61, 76
Boliver, Vikki 29, 99
boundary/ies: blurring of 21, 54, 65; objects 21–23; spanning 25–27, 58–61; structures 23–25, 57–59; theory 4–9, 14–16, 27, 30–34, 90–95; *see also* transaction(s)

capital 68; human 26, 34, 49; scientific 48, 70; social 14, 34, 45, 50, 70
careers 25, 53, 59, 71
Cell, John W. 15
chemistry 5, 25, 29, 59, 76
Clark, Burton R. 24, 30, 90
collaboration 20–21, 45, 54–55, 74–75, 81, 83; with industry 17, 22, 26, 60, 68, 87–88
computer science 40, 52, 70, 90, 97
Considine, Mark 90

departments 48, 55, 57–58, 60, 65–66, 92; in sample 29–30, 74–76, 81–85, 87–88, 94
disciplinarity 8, 15–18, 33–34, 49, 67–68, 84–87; transdisciplinarity 23–25, 46, 48, 57–58, 74–75
Douglas, Mary 84
Durkheim, Émile 25, 67, 86

engineering 29, 46, 60, 67, 75, 86
entrepreneurial/ship 1, 27, 34; commercialising 26, 44–45; consulting 48, 58, 86; patenting 22–23, 26, 45, 55; spin-outs 23, 26, 47–48, 58; university 23, 90–92
environmental science 29, 45–47, 56–57, 60, 69, 86
Etzkowitz, Henry 90–91

Index

graduates 5–6, 17–18, 26–27, 53, 59, 63–66, 87–88

higher education 18, 26–27, 64, 81, 90

impact 20, 30–34, 57, 74, 84–85; agenda 2–4, 24, 67, 86, 93–94; impactful research 28, 48, 50–52, 59–61, 80, 91; perceptions of 82–83

knowledge: codified 25–26, 34, 44–45, 65; domains 5, 14–16, 64, 80; exchange 33, 50, 71; as 'invisible material' 30; regimes 63, 73–76; society 2, 63, 66, 77, 86, 91; tacit 25–26, 34; transfer 4, 6, 23, 25–26, 58; users of 19–23, 31–33, 45, 55–57, 74–75, 81–86

mathematics 29, 55, 59, 76
McNie, Elizabeth 31, 47
medicine 29, 43–44, 48–50, 54, 57, 71
Mode 2 68, 73–75, 92
Moore, Rob 71

New Public Management 3
Nowotny, Helga 24, 75

OECD Centre for Educational Research and Innovation (CERI) 5, 19, 23–24, 26
outputs 6, 17–18, 20–23, 44, 55; journals 17, 32, 44–45, 47–48, 50; publications 17, 22, 33, 55–56, 58, 70
outreach 18–19, 23, 31, 34, 46–47, 51–54

physics 5, 15–16, 29, 43, 48, 53, 55, 76
Polanyi, Michael 25
psychological sciences 29, 48–50, 56, 61, 86
public engagement 47, 49, 52, 70

research: activity 6–8, 54–56, 81–82, 85–89; aims, goals and objectives 20–22, 32–33, 43–44, 46, 57–58, 72–73, 85–86; assessment and evaluation 3, 32; case studies of 43–50; centres 4, 6, 23, 30, 43, 45, 59; councils 3, 45; funding and sponsorship 8, 19, 26, 46–48, 68, 81–82; orientation 8, 28–29, 55, 81, 84–86, 89; policy 2–3, 18, 22, 24, 27, 80, 93; problem-oriented 23; Research Excellence Framework (REF) 3, 28–29, 50, 80, 82–83, 94; units 23–24, 30, 45–48, 58–59, 65

science: branches of 28–29, 77, 81, 87–90; postacademic 21, 55, 74–75, 92; STEMM 8, 26, 64, 80, 91, 94
Shields, Robin 91
Slaughter, Sheila 22, 26
sociology 5, 14, 23, 27, 68, 90
Stokes, Donald 29
students 18, 23, 25–27, 48, 53, 58–60, 65–66, 68, 84; teaching of 2, 51–53, 57–61, 63–65, 77, 84, 86; *see also* graduates

technology 22–26, 44–48, 55–56, 74–76, 84–85; technology transfer *see* knowledge, transfer
technoscience 9, 73, 75–76, 92
third mission 2–3, 19–20, 23–24, 26, 51–53, 57, 84–86
transaction(s) 5–6, 16–19, 42–43, 45–48, 50–51; transaction costs 16–17, 64–65, 83–84
Trowler, Paul 90

university: history of 25, 67–68; as institution 1–9, 55, 66–68, 81, 91, 93–94; 'ivory tower' 5, 16; management 1, 3, 7, 24; sector 20–21, 63–65, 80–81, 90, 92, 95
use-inspired basic 29, 48, 55–56, 84–86, 93; *see also* research, orientation

Vakkuri, Jarmo 19

Watermeyer, Richard 91

Ziman, John 92

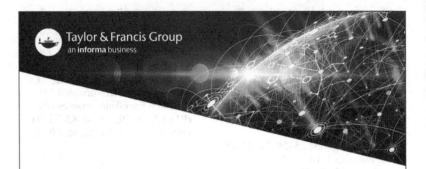

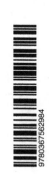